WILFRID SHEED

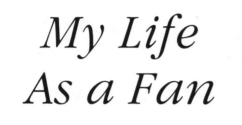

*My Life
As a Fan*

SIMON & SCHUSTER
New York London Toronto Sydney
Tokyo Singapore

SIMON & SCHUSTER
SIMON & SCHUSTER BUILDING
ROCKEFELLER CENTER
1230 AVENUE OF THE AMERICAS
NEW YORK, NEW YORK 10020

DESIGNED BY EVE METZ
MANUFACTURED IN THE UNITED STATES OF AMERICA

10 9 8 7 6 5 4 3 2 1

LIBRARY OF CONGRESS CATALOGING-IN-PUBLICATION DATA

SHEED, WILFRID.
    MY LIFE AS A FAN/WILFRID SHEED.
        P.   CM.
    1. SHEED, WILFRID.   2. BASEBALL FANS—UNITED STATES—
BIOGRAPHY.   3. FOOTBALL FANS—UNITED STATES—
BIOGRAPHY.   4. BASEBALL—UNITED STATES—HISTORY—20TH
CENTURY.   5. FOOTBALL—UNITED STATES—HISTORY—20TH
CENTURY.   I. TITLE.
GV865.S455A3   1993
796.357'092—DC20   92-38021
[B]   CIP

ISBN 0-671-76710-0

Contents

Author's Note

THIS IS A BOOK OF MEMORIES not facts, which means that while I'm convinced it happened exactly like this, I wouldn't advise using the book to settle bar bets. *The Baseball Encyclopedia* has its memories and I have mine, and if by ill chance we differ on some small point, I've had mine much too long and they're much too vivid to change them now.

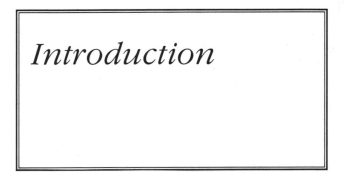

Introduction

Graham Greene used to call some of his books "entertainments," and it's a word that would come in handy right now, except that claiming it for one's own work has always had a kind of a funny ring to American, or even Americanized, ears. What the author seems to be saying is "Of *course* this book will entertain you, but I could be doing so much more." To which the best answer would probably be what Oscar Levant said when Eddie left Debbie to marry Liz: "How could he stoop so high?" I for one would give my front seat at the next New York Mets World Series to be sure I had written an entertainment.

Nothing sounds quite as arrogant as English apology, but

then again no one is as quick to suspect arrogance every time the dog barks as an American, and Mr. Greene may not have meant that at all, but something more like "Unfortunately, my novels won't entertain you at all, but perhaps this one will just a little bit." Having been the victim of more than a few transatlantic misunderstandings myself, I would like tentatively to call what follows an entertainment in the second, mock-humble sense—an entertainment plus a little something.

To begin at the beginning. When I was a youth, before the great trivia boom and the comic-book bubble, normal healthy little eggheads (and in my family, you were an egghead until proved otherwise) were assumed to have too much going on in their crania to have any cells left for the boxed-in, horizonless world of sports. Maybe a little rock climbing in New Hampshire would have been acceptable, or hiking through the Berkshires, or how about some competitive sonnet writing? but skip that organized, regimented, uncreative stuff that you play with teams and rules and dreary old balls. ("*I* know, why not a square ball? or an octagon?" "Cuthbert, you slay me!")

So imagine my horror at finding I was not just interested in sports but consumed by them. It was like discovering a squint or a hidden deformity. Your parents heartily assured themselves that you would outgrow it in time along with your short pants and pimples. But then another year would go by and another and they'd find you squinting worse than ever. So maybe you weren't an egghead after all, huh, please?

In my case, unfortunately, that would have made for a lonely sort of life as I went shuffling off every night, tolling my bell, to the arms of my *Who's Who in Baseball* and my *Pro Football Roundup*. "My son the sports fan." My son the half-wit.

INTRODUCTION

Thank God I developed some other interests in time, and was consumed by those too, and was even able to make a species of career out of writing about them. Because there was no question in those days of using that other stuff, all the RBIs and the earned run averages that had burned their way through my early years. Other writers could mine their childhoods to a fare-thee-well: the summers by the shore, the elm tree at your aunt's house that they had to cut down and nothing was ever the same, or the day you discovered grandfather's ear trumpet with the swastikas on it—why, you might even get fifteen volumes or so out of some old piece of French pastry that rubbed you the right way. It seemed that any old fluff would do for literature so long as it was pre- or semiconscious enough. Sports itself could be made to do if you kept it sufficiently vague and suggestive. Holding your dad's hand at the fathers-and-sons softball game, for instance, and it felt clammy by the seventh inning and he smelled funny now, and you began to cry. But *hold the batting averages!*

The worst of it was that I half agreed. By cutting through the murk of impressions that fogs in childhood, sports also cuts you off, even more decisively than learning to read does, from the primal, unmediated material that is yours alone, the only story you have to tell at this point, and makes you instead a somewhat dense adult, a miniature book-keeper, all at sea among the names and numbers of the grown-up world. A child's first drawing, or his first full sen-tence, may still be interesting thirty years later, but his thoughts on the current pennant race, like his opinion of the next election, will just be a bad imitation of a grown-up opinion and not worth saving.

So there they sat for years, the hours spent mulling and brooding, living and dying over various sports, adding up to a monument the size of a small city to wasted time and attention. Other writers might have gold deposits stashed all around their backyards, but I just had this heap of slag at the bottom of mine. Which should teach me a lesson about starting to think too early in life. Where I should have been gazing at a madeleine and letting the associations roll, I had been munching knowingly on a hot dog and wondering like any old barfly how many teams had ever come from eight games behind in mid-August, or how many points higher Stan Musial might have hit if he hadn't met a coach with a warped sense of humor who'd taught him to stand that way at the plate. And I defy even Marcel "Corky" Proust to get fifteen volumes out of *that*.

Yet from time to time I would gaze wistfully at my slag heap twinkling in the sun and ask myself whether it might not be worth at least *something?* There was an awful lot of raw experience in there, much of it radioactively intense and impossible to dispose of. None of the normal kids I knew seemed to have ever come within light miles of the rich, billowing sorrow I felt when the Cardinals passed the Dodgers in 1942: an adult causing such pain to a child would be put away somewhere. Yet between the last Sunday and Wednesday of September that year I would find myself sufficiently recovered from that devastating but totally artificial and make-believe pain to enjoy the Cardinals' victory over the Yankees that October as much as I've ever enjoyed a World Series any time, with a special blend of mellowness laced with rue that also seemed quite alien to my regular friends. The wounds of the season had suddenly washed away like greasepaint, to be replaced by the face of a happy clown.

There was, to be sure, much bad and boring logic in that head as well, and half-baked opinion, but there was a quirkiness and force of emotion that seem to flatten out as you grow older. As the material in this book draws closer to the present, I find myself turning more and more into just another fan, with a clearer, more judicious mind than before, but of a sort that might belong to anybody. When I go to a ballpark these days, I probably see pretty much what everybody else sees there, and have no story all my own to tell afterwards.

Back then it was different. In what seemed like the vast wastes of Shibe Park in 1941, I must, just for openers, have been the only kid on hand with short pants and an English accent whose family had left England just before the German bombs came looking for us (our house was hit later and so was my father's office) and who didn't yet understand or much like anything about America except for this gorgeous beautiful game.

But even if I hadn't been any of those things, my experience would still have been different from yours because, as I've been discovering in conversation, no two sports biographies are exactly alike, any more than any two musical biographies are exactly alike. The friend you first went to a game with was different, and so was the adult who laid down the law and got everything wrong, misleading you for years, and so were the sights and the smells and the things that would stick in your mind forever (who else in the world still cares that Wally Moses held the bat as if he were about to drop it?) and the things you'd miss completely, like the fact that you'd been watching a no-hitter that day. And all the differences were magnified to the point of weirdness by their sheer novelty. This might be one of the last times you would ever find yourself looking at a picture in which every single detail was new to you.

So what was it *like?* This is the question that literature begins with, and most baseball books end before they get to. I remember no greater frustration while growing up than saving pennies to buy a sports book, possibly written or "told to" by a great athlete who has seen everything, and finding this question unanswered and unconsidered. After Mickey Owen dropped the third strike, who said what in the Dodger clubhouse? And in the other one: did DiMaggio smile for once or conceivably snap a towel at Henrich— well, probably what they really did was get down on their knees and offer a World Series goat to Baal, the Yankee god who lived on flesh and flannel. Hence, "Take me out to the . . ."—no, I can't go on with this. Don Honig's magnificent baseball interview books (*Baseball When the Grass Was Real,* etc.) soared immediately above the field because they did answer the question for this and that player at this and that time; and Jim Brosnan's *The Long Season* answered it a bit more, and Jim Bouton's *Ball Four* answered it a lot more. But that still left and still leaves an ocean of sports experience out there.

And in the stands as well. Go to Cooperstown sometime, or just open an old baseball book, and look at some of the crowd pictures. You can usually tell what era you're in right away by the kinds of hats the men are wearing, or in our own hatless times, by the number of women in the stands, which has grown from none at all—making the stands a locker room unto themselves—to enough to change the whole atmosphere in some sections, and the *sound* of a ball game.

One picture that has stuck in my mind for so long that I can't even remember where I first saw it features a bunch of merry fellows in derbies clambering to the top of a wooden fence (there must have been some hellacious fist-fights off camera) to watch Walter Johnson confronting the latest rage, Smokey Joe Wood. What are they *saying?* If one could just turn the sound up for a second, one would hear what Virginia Woolf called (in reference to Ring Lardner)

"the voice of a continent." Or follow them to the saloon
later on, and pick up the sound there—the group roar and
the stray shout. *He didn't look that fast to me, are you
kidding, Jaysus. Stick it in your hat* (or whatever they were
saying that year). And home quietly afterwards. "You promised to take the kids." "Stick it in your hat." Or in the ideal
home of the period: "Did you have a nice time, dear?"
"Jaysus. You've never seen anything like it."

Rich material in any era. But the catch is that you have to
be interested in, or at least tolerant of, the language of
baseball. Otherwise it's just talk. And that was the real, non-
negotiable problem with my own memories. There is no
way I can now extract the essence of them for the basebally
illiterate (or should it be basebally-challenged?) without en-
cumbering these readers with a few baseball details; no way
I can convey how it felt to have my heart shattered like a
walnut by the Cardinals in '42 and then rebuilt by them
without giving at least some idea of what the Cardinals did
on the diamond that year.

And the same goes for the half-baked opinions I formed
about those details, which by now are part of the details. It
is never enough for a baseball fan to suffer, he must also
talk. In fact, to feel *is* to talk. So even though the pain of
losing that year was, like all pain, elemental and speechless,
it was encrusted in chatter all the way. How could a team
win 104 games and lose the pennant? How could a team
whose top home run hitter gets exactly 13 dingers win *106*
games in the lively ball era? And where, when you come
right down to it, does a guy get off having a name like
Creepy Crespi anyway? Some of the phrases I used back
then may sound suspiciously precocious, but they were the
phrases going around, and we *all* used them, regardless of
age. And still do. When the blissful time comes to take my

grandson to a ball game, we will not need an interpreter, any more than I needed one with the graybeards of my own era.

Indeed, as I review what I've written in here (trivia question: has any introduction *ever* been written before the book?), I find the image returning to me again and again of an older man sitting in the stands with a child, surprised at times by how much the lad knows about this game since he doesn't seem to know that much of anything else—and the records say he's a scrupulously average student—but then again amused at how he can get things so wrong from time to time. Occasionally, the old-timer can take no more of it, and butts in to set the kid straight about something. But generally speaking the conversation just flows back and forth, so that by the end of the day, neither of them can remember for sure which said what.

Baseball may be unique among sports in the sheer amount of solid matter it gives a child's mind to cut its teeth on. But the more I sat here, pencil in mouth, watching my early self chewing away and groping toward rational thought, the more he seemed like a stranger, until by the time he returned to England in 1946 with the stamp of baseball all over him, like a suitcase that's only been to ballparks, he seemed like a fictional character altogether. So I foraged around among names for him that suggested Englishness, Irishness, and baseball but finally settled on a device dear to middle European novelists of naming him after a letter, such as K or X—except that the letter I chose is "I," which I understand has a double meaning in English.

So much the better, since "I" shares my experiences and thoughts so closely: but be warned, he also slips off the tracks into fiction every so often. Insofar as I can remember my thoughts and sensations at that age, they're in here faithfully—but there's always something missing in such memories, a core-self that keeps childishness from seeming silly at the time to the person involved, and this tends to get replaced, however hard you try, with adult condescension. A kid reading a grown-up's account of him would boil over with tears and indignation. "It wasn't like that at all!"

Objection noted and sympathized with. However, I never expect to get closer to my old self than I have in this book, and for a particular reason. Nineteen eighty-eight, the year it was conceived, was a bad one for me, with various irritations mental, physical, and professional spurring each other on and contriving to leave me in a state best described as suspended convalescence. And during this strange time, I suddenly found myself enjoying baseball, and to a lesser extent football, almost as much as I had as a child, and looking forward to each game like a convict on visitors day, and I decided to celebrate the greatest of all sports (with a friendly nod to football) one way or another the minute I got better.

Since then I have returned to an amnesiac normal, and baseball has resumed its usual place in my concerns—which is to say, I'm rabid when I think about it (there are some things that are not worth doing calmly), but I doubt if I could still name sixteen major-league lineups as quickly wide awake as I could in my sleep back in 1941, and if I were asked to go abroad in, say, June, I don't imagine I would cling to the bedpost and refuse to budge.

But I believe I captured the memories, and this book, just in time.

1

Year One: The View from the Attic

One of the more serious losses of the last fifty years has been, without doubt, the great American attic. Anyone who ever had the good luck to live in, or seriously visit, an old house will remember the pleasure of clumping up the stairs and killing a gorgeous afternoon or so in one of those caverns of wonder, built appropriately overhead rather than underfoot in the Old World style for burying treasure. The air smelled strange and different up there—people said it needed an airing, but that was the last thing it needed—and there was *always* a surprise waiting, in the form of a book, a lithograph, a sled, a funny-looking hat, or in my case, evidence of a great sport played around here in this very century. Hours later when you came clumping down again, people could tell from the look in your eye that you'd been in the attic—a look of wistful astonishment and of sheer how-the-hell-did-that-get-there? that even the best-endowed museums and libraries despair of inspiring. Like a random number in math, the jumble in a good attic could never have been planned, because no sane person thinks like that.

This will not, however, be a history of American housing except in this one sense, that people who grew up in the attic era are likely to think of this particular room as a more and more satisfactory image of how their own minds work and also as a natural place for voyages to begin. It was as simple as going to the movies, and indeed the movies worked the image pretty much to death as soon as they thought of it back in the forties. You simply picked up some object and stared at it and the years rolled back and the seasons changed. And you knew if you looked out the window, you'd see a horse and buggy in the driveway or a Ford V-8, or in my case a 1940 De Soto with Dr. Daley pumping the horn and yelling to come on down, you're going to miss the kickoff.

Nineteen forty was, by chance, the year my baseball *and* American football lives began: in other words, the year I came to America, aged nine, dragging my family behind me. The country was fairly honeycombed with attics in those days. Ranch houses and split-levels had not yet sprung up like toadstools and it was quite possible for a nine-year-old refugee to attic-hop his way across the county like John Cheever's swimmer, acquiring a crazy-quilt education along the way, from a Civil War uniform and rusty bayonet here to a stack of Superman comics there. Since most of the physical objects required an adult along to explain, and only very old adults had the time and patience (and they had too much), your best bet was print, which went at your own speed for as long as you wanted.

So I would untie the string and plow my way with the doggedness of a German research scholar through back numbers of *Life* and *Reader's Digest* and of course everywhere the *National Geographic,* which seemed to be left around as an educational tool (if you must learn about women's chests, let it be in the dullest possible surroundings).

Since we were parked just outside Philadelphia, the *Saturday Evening Post* really *was* everywhere, like hotel Bibles, and it was there that I discovered baseball, in the mythic form of a picture of a fat man lying on his side like a beached whale or perhaps, since he was trussed in catcher's regalia, more like an extra-large knight buried in his armor, while another man lay on his back a few feet away with his legs splayed gracefully in what I now take to have been a perfect hook slide. Ernie Lombardi, explained the text, was "swooning," though the man in the picture looked too heavy to move, awake *or* asleep, while the graceful fellow next to him was the great Joe DiMaggio himself (everyone knew *that* name), scoring the conclusive run in a World Series game.

Again and again I returned to this picture: it wasn't much of a representation of baseball—as a first glimpse, it was about on a par with the view of a great city you get while driving from the airport. But it hooked me, and I read the whole story through, absorbing forever names like Charley Keller and Paul Derringer and Bill McKechnie. And I still can think of no better reason why teachers should get paid more. Here you had an average sort of schoolboy's memory, which had routinely resisted all the information they threw at me in class, suddenly swinging open at a touch to absorb and almost drown in the likes of Lonnie Frey and Billy Werber, and I still didn't know what it was exactly that they did, except that it was some version of the game I saw occasionally from train windows—a game too jerky and inept at that level to be beautiful, but quite compelling, and clearly a game with my name on it.

My other piece of attic lore that first year concerned Hank Greenberg, "baseball's most eligible bachelor," a dashing-looking fellow in a dinner jacket, who had once paid local kids dimes and quarters (I pictured them as about my size, though they were probably young giants) to throw to him as he set sail for the home run record in 1938. A picture of Hammering Hank the bachelor, playing out his eligibility with—could it have been a debutante? could it have been his future wife? could I have invented the whole thing?—merges in my mind with an ad for Goodrich tires, featuring various other Detroit Tigers frolicking in Lakeland, Florida. In one frame, the boys were sprawled over and around a jalopy covered in graffiti. "Bored of education" is the only one I remember, but they all had that same shirttail-out, slap-happy quality that still wins foreigners to America if they're going to be won by anything. The palm trees in the ad looked particularly fine to me, as we dug in for our first winter of checking thermostats in the frozen North, but they were just part of the rich baseball life, with its dinner jackets and laughing players and year-round sunshine. Since I *still* wasn't entirely sure what these guys did, I couldn't swear that I didn't dream of becoming a ballplayer out of season before I dreamed of becoming one in.

Perhaps at nine, you are going to fall in love with the first sport that comes along, just as at seventeen you're pretty much obligated to break your heart. I can only say that baseball was not without competition in the winter of 1940–41. The sport actually being played at the moment was football, and what's more, I had seen a game. The ever-obliging Dr. Joe Daley had driven me into Philadelphia to see the Eagles humiliated—all Philadelphia teams were humiliated in those days, on sight, and who knows how that affected one's view of the city? Defeat brought out the worst in Philadelphia fans, but then, I'm told, so does victory.

Anyhow, the instrument of humiliation that day was Byron "Whizzer" White of the Lions, who bucked the line for three touchdowns, and probably learned a thing or two about "cruel and unusual punishment" as well from watching what his teammates did to the shrimpy Davey O'Brien of the Eagles. Years later Justice Byron R. White would write an important opinion pronouncing that the death penalty was *always* cruel and unusual: but so was playing tailback for Philadelphia before they went to the T-formation in 1942 and began to look like professionals.

The outcome of this game was dozens of crayon drawings from me of football players running and tackling, which my mother as usual found promising. Since I couldn't remember anything my sister or I ever did that my mother did *not* find promising, the praise did not go to my head. What *did* go to my head that fall (and I wouldn't have thought of it if I hadn't used that very phrase) was the flying shoe of a runner I was trying to tackle from behind one day after school. I guess I must have assured the handful of guys who were left on the playground that I felt okay, yessir, and I wandered off smartly in the general direction of home, and when I got there it was pitch-dark and everyone was waiting anxiously on the porch. Where in the world had I been? "By the creek" was all I could remember—which was strange, because the creek was a good half mile in the wrong direction; what I remembered more clearly was unparalleled misery and confusion, as if half of my brain had tumbled, or been jammed, into the other half. Probably "a mild concussion," said Dr. Daley the next day—mother of God, what could a serious one feel like? Anyway, welcome to football.

The episode did not put me off football in the least. Stick to touch football, said my elders—but what was the fun of that? Cause and effect reveal themselves slowly and haltingly at that age, and it was years before I associated the pain of that afternoon with the routine and inevitable battlefield damage of football. It still looked like a hell of a game to me.

It just wasn't so interesting to read about as baseball. The *Saturday Evening Post* allotted its space with metronomic fairness to both sports, but outside of a piece about mousetrap blocking (they didn't call it the draw play yet), I can't remember a word of their football stuff. For that game, *Life,* with its bang-bang pictures and brief grunts of text, was my source—in particular an issue of it which seemed to sit in our downstairs bathroom for weeks and weeks and which contained pictures of Tommy Harmon having his shirt shredded by Pennsylvania tacklers as he raced past them. I don't know if the University of Michigan had designed the shirts expressly for him, but they were an artist's delight, and nearly all the drawings that my mother found so promising were either versions of Harmon running around and looking like an early Christian martyr, with Pennsylvania tacklers clutching at him and Forest Evashevski blocking, or else of someone like Davey O'Brien throwing to Don Freitag, the Michigan end. Again the names swarmed into my memory unopposed by the formidable blocking that had that very fall kept out (and still keeps out) the names of the Presidents and the signers of the Declaration. I don't know, maybe history teachers should be paid *less,* because at that age, I seemed to remember *everything* but schoolwork and where I'd left my gloves. Although foot-

ball names were no match for such majestic baseball han-
dles as Enos Slaughter and Estel Crabtree and Coaker
Triplett, I find I still recall six of them from the 1940 All-
American football team, although I only saw a couple of the
names once for maybe five minutes in another copy of *Life*.
Jack Kimbrough I knew, because he had helped Texas A&M
to beat Fordham in the Cotton Bowl (who can forget Lou
Filipowiz and Blacky Blumenstock?), but Tom Sufferage of
Tennessee? and Augie Leo of Georgetown? Give me (as we
didn't yet say) a break. And where the heck was Frank Rea-
gan of Penn?

The Reagan issue in fact loomed over all the other football issues that year, because to judge from the local press,
this was one of the two or three greatest football players of
all time: yet he didn't even rate *Life* magazine's second-
string backfield. It would take me a couple of more years to
adjust the focus and see local heroes as the minnows they
usually were in the larger scheme of things (after which the
temptation became to underrate them). As it was, I felt that
a monstrous injustice had been done to a very great man.
Although I had never seen Reagan personally, the Horans
across town spoke well of him, and who knew better than
the Horans?

What makes children the rich comic characters that they
are is their uncanny sense of perspective. For several more
years, for instance, I would believe that Adelphi College
must be a major power because it came at the beginning of
a football guide I picked up once. And if Adelphi was so
hot, could Pratt and Upsala be far behind?

It was all the same to my English mother and Australian
father, while to the few other small boys in the neighborhood it didn't matter a damn either way.

One of the first things even the most obtuse sports fanatic
cottons to right away is that he is "different," a deviant, but

a harmless one. Unlike intellectuals and homosexuals, he has a place in the gang, though a humble one like a court jester's. "Ask Sheed—he knows everything." You have to be a little weird to know all that stuff, and weird can never be the best thing to be, but you're all right, you've turned your powers to benign, good-guy purposes. "What do you do, sit up all night and study that stuff?" There is no right answer to this, but you're probably better off with "Yes." It's better to be a crank than a genius. Otherwise you can try "It's just a knack," and try to make up for it with dreadful school-work.

None of this really mattered that winter, because there were so few guys in the village of Torresdale, Pennsylvania, that we had to take each other on any terms we could get: in such isolation, who could tell who was normal or weird around here anyway? But I would learn the ethos with a vengeance the next winter in boarding school, where you jockey with your elbows just for a place in the pack.

One last football bulletin, before we plunge into a sport-less winter and rattle around in the dark for a while and out again into sunlight and the best sport ever devised by man. There was no alternative to the *New York Times* at our place, although later in the day you could catch glimpses of the *Philadelphia Inquirer* and the *Bulletin* on other people's porches (I became a master at reading upside down), and so it was in that tedious, comicless paper, which repre-sented everything that was worst about the word "grown-up," that I read one Sunday that the Chicago Bears were about to play the Washington Redskins for the champion-ship that very afternoon.

My eye fixed on the pictures of the two starting teams—which were also the finishing teams in those days, so you didn't need a wide lens for the team photo. Osmanski, McAfee, Turner, Luckman—the names didn't mean a thing

23

to me yet, though later they would spring to life, and com-
mence running around in a corner of my brain forever and
ever: the playground area behind the music rack. On the
Redskin side, I noted the name Justice, which struck me as
a swell name for a football player, and on the strength of
that, and the fact that the Redskins had beaten these same
guys two weeks earlier, I decided to root for Washington
that afternoon.

And then the roof fell in. The Bears' score that afternoon
was one of several typographical errors I have suspected in
my years as a fan (the whole month of September, 1951, as
reported in the London *Daily Express,* is another, as we'll
see—what do the Brits know about baseball?). 73–0 was
simply impossible. You couldn't *do* that in football. I stamp
my foot in memory. I knew football scores, and in those
days 14–0 was a trouncing and 21–0 was a rout. 73–0 was a
bad joke, which would presumably be atoned for in later
issues of the Monday *Times.*

But the newsreels at the local moviehouse bore out this
ridiculous outcome and, with time, I came to accept it. Years
later, my six-year-old son would insist that there were only
two outs in a Yankees–Twins game we were watching and
that the fielding team should be ordered to resume their
positions immediately. And it was no use telling him that
four umpires and fifty players disagreed with him. So it runs
in the family.

In retrospect, the choppy black-and-white newsreels of
that miserable game now remind me of nothing so much
as old pornographic movies in which the directors seemed
to run the same few centimeters of film over and over to
make a quickie into an epic. But it could also have been an
instructional film on how the newfangled T-formation
worked, not to mention an irresistible commercial for it.

For the first time in the dour, character-building history

of American football, the possibility of scoring on any play from any part of the field had been broached, and the game would never be the same. The small world of football, which in those days went out of existence like the village of Brigadoon for three-quarters of the year, was knocked sideways by the quick strikes of Osmanski and the long-range bombs of Luckman, and some of this excitement gradually filtered through to my mental attic where the events of 1940 were already being stacked for future reference. In May, it had been the Germans' turn, slicing through France in the form of fierce black arrows streaking across the map—*slam* through the Ardennes, *bam* through the Vosges, and thank you ma'am in Paris itself. Now the maps showed McAfee off tackle and Scooter McLean around end.

Okay—my sense of proportion wasn't *that* bad, I knew football wasn't *really* important. Life in our village went on pretty much as normal after the game, and my parents didn't seem to realize that anything had happened at all. But in the backwoods of the psyche, things are not always so clear. On film, nothing has ever looked so black or ominous as the Bears' uniforms that day, and calling them the "Monsters of the Midway" only made it worse. Earlier that year I had seen pictures of the Nazi panzer divisions, and frankly I thought these guys could take them. In a fair fight, of course.

The experience of sports can be blindingly intense such that at its peak even a grown-up can't always be sure what's important and what isn't. Just last summer I slammed my fist so hard on the dashboard of my car when a Mets relief pitcher gave up a totally UNNECESSARY home run that my hand rang all the way to the elbow. I've taken bad reviews more calmly; in fact, I've taken earthquakes and wars more calmly. Strength of response, as one learns eventually, has only a hit-or-miss connection with what really matters to you. But try telling that to a nine-year-old. My hard-bitten baseball coach, Father Felix Pepin, cried like a baby when Barry Fitzgerald clapped eyes on his aging mom in *Going My Way* until I thought I'd have to help him out of the theater, and I would have felt shocked and betrayed to know how soon he probably got over it.

As it works out, sports help you to learn these lessons faster than anything can by forcing you to act them out so foolishly and often. On that Monday, for instance, I was stunned by the Bears' score, and then again on Saturday when we all went to the movies, and then yet again when I saw the monsters in the flesh two years later, administering yet another pounding, this time to the Eagles. But in between those dates, they meant nothing to me at all: sports have so many other griefs to attend to and joys to celebrate that every time your heart is on the brink of breaking, you find yourself jerked away from the graveside to attend yet another funeral or wedding.

The Bears game turned out to be a very mild inoculation for the truly serious sorrows of summer. What, after all, did I care what happened to the Redskins? Just a few years later, I would have said "Justice didn't triumph" and cackled. As it was, I filed the whole thing away under "bullies that get away with it," a huge file that year, and turned my attention to the next sport—above which, smirking haughtily, sat perhaps the most terrifying monsters of all.

Within the next few years, to paraphrase Ira Gershwin, the Bears would tumble and the panzers would crumble, but the New York Yankees would still be up there a good quarter century later, keeping my "bullies" file open and warping my view of reality until I was too old to change it.

It is a lasting regret of mine that I saw no good basketball that winter, but saw, if anything, almost the opposite. On my way home from school, I sometimes dropped in on my sister's school, which was partway there, for a breather. And there I naturally found a ball game (I could find one anywhere): at first the field hockey of autumn, where I could swear I once saw one of the Kennedy girls laying waste on all sides, and later basketball, where I was much taken by a guard named Betty Bush. Just turned ten, I did not believe in girls yet, but I was taken with this one anyway, and watched her to the near exclusion of everything else.

One gains ground in some areas, but loses it in others, and a season spent staring at something other than sports was not such a bad idea then or now; in fact, it could be that I owe everything else I have to the basketball season.

Be that as it may, the game remains a poor relation among my sports enthusiasms. Watching Bill Russell of the Boston Celtics at Madison Square Garden one night, I could only wish fervently that I'd seen something like this sooner —I could have watched Russell sweeping the boards and starting the next play, all in one motion, forever. But of course, there wasn't anything like that sooner. Early 1940s basketball wasn't really a spectator sport at all, and anyone caught playing like Russell or his flashy teammate Bob Cousy would probably have been sent off the court for doing *something* wrong, we'll think of what in a moment: basketball just wasn't supposed to look like that.

But the big discovery of that first winter was snow, that great gift of the North American climate. Unlike the scraggly bits of it you sometimes saw in England, this stuff was opulent and decisive and it sat there forever in those days (maybe it still does but not where I live) like a print on the wall, occasionally punctuated by roving bands of small boys whooping it up and horsing around.

But I found it wasn't that easy to decide exactly what to do with snow. My parents gave me a sled, which was standard issue for country kids, but since there wasn't anything that could faintly be described as a hill in Torresdale—and since even the Swedes hadn't yet figured a way to make a sport out of sledding on flat ground—my Flexible Flyer would have to wait for a year. The other thing you learn quickly in any part of the country is that once you've built one snowman, you've built them all (alias Timmy O'Malley once tried to equip a snowman with sexual parts, which would have been different, but they kept falling off) and the same goes for destroying them. So the best bet seemed to be either to throw it or wrestle in it, and I was mighty tired of both by springtime. In fact, it's possible that all those bands of small boys were running around out of sheer boredom and desperation long before the winter relented and skulked offstage.

The long, cold American winter plays into baseball's hands in several ways, the most obvious being that you are going to welcome just about any sport that comes along at that point, especially one with a whole summer up its sleeve; but a subtler one being the sheer pleasure of staying home by the fire, or in the attic, and thinking about it. In those pre-television days, a sports fan couldn't just summon with a jaded flip of the wrist lush images of the Hawaiian Open or Pebble Beach to take the curse off February: he had to remember and imagine it all on his own, using for memories any scrap he could get his hands on, be it a picture of Tigers in Lakeland or a paragraph about Joe DiMaggio's contract difficulties. Or even a photo of a catcher fast asleep beside the plate.

Obviously, this is harder to do if you don't have anything to remember yet—but it's not impossible with this particular sport, which must be about the only one ever devised that can grab your interest when you have neither seen it nor played it yourself. (Years later my son, who had just learned how to read, greeted me at breakfast with the words "Guess what, Dad, Moe Drabowsky's ERA was 3.54 last year," and all he had seen so far were bubble-gum cards.) Although, contrariwise, I *had* seen football played about as well as it could be in those days, it had only a small lead in my mind over this other sport, sight unseen. So I was ripe for the taking when the days finally got longer and the snowbanks dwindled into honest-to-God grass and the country was fit for real, instead of imaginary, baseball once again.

Before I leave attics for good, though, I'd like to mention one last one which I stumbled upon years later and which seemed to sum up the whole experience and may incidentally have set this book in motion. The year was 1975, and I was on the West Coast, negotiating over a book on Muhammad Ali which I hoped to subtitle "School Bills" in honor of the chief reason I would be writing it. (Not that I didn't love boxing and Ali too, but there were novels to be written, and sports at that time seemed like a gorgeous woman beckoning me into a blind alley. Also, it was to be a quickie picture book, which meant I would just be holding up slides and doing the patter.)

It is just this type of humdrum, no-big-deal pressure that attics were probably put on earth to relieve. After a couple of weeks of jousting in polo lounges and executive suites, the smell and crackle of old magazines were as welcome as a gleam of water on the desert. My wife and I had repaired to San Francisco, which is kind of an attic unto itself, and it was there that I found the best of all possible ones in the house of some old dear friends.

Just one item, if it's simply perfect, can put an attic over the top, and the item in this case was a bound collection of *PM* newspapers for the whole of July 1940, which was by chance also my first month in this country.

Henry James probably would have liked a different word for every possible sensation in life, even if only one person has experienced it only once. My sensation as I read those old newspapers was almost of that kind: pungent and distinct enough to deserve a name, but too rare ever to get it. It is the sensation you get from reading what was happening all around you while you were a year or so too young to realize it—and not from reading about it in a history book, but through the clucks and squawks of a daily paper. Yogi Berra's phrase "déjà vu all over again" comes close, but lacks precision.

That July was a busy little month, as it turns out, what with Wendell Willkie coming from way back on the outside to burst through the pack in one of the last Republican conventions that could truly be compared with a horse race, and the German army, using its hurry-up offense, doing what used to be considered a whole war's worth of work in a few weeks as they mopped up France.

But I knew the broad outlines of those things already. What really leapt from the page were two pictorial spreads: the lesser one showing close-up pictures of a German panzer division going about its business and taken by an American photographer from behind enemy lines, reminding one with a start of how very neutral this country still was as Europe fell; but the pile driver being a full center-spread entitled "Our Phantom Fleet," depicting all of Uncle Sam's Pacific battleships, which according to the text, skimmed that ocean like gray ghosts, defying any enemy to find them, let alone enemies with buckteeth and thick glasses. You'll recognize the names right away: the U.S.S. *Arizona,* the

California, the *Pennsylvania*—all the phantoms that later turned up in one basket and were mowed down in less than a morning at Pearl Harbor.

I turned as one did at the time to the sports pages for relief, and it was there that I found the gem, the item that sets you off on your own private moon shot and makes an attic an attic. "Bob Bowman beans Ducky Medwick" is not a headline guaranteed to stir the blood of just anyone, but to those in the know it spoke for the kind of event that makes you wonder just what you were doing at the moment it happened.

That beaning was the opening shot in a war that would proceed to involve me and stretch my puny emotional range for the next few years a good deal more than the real war was able to. War can make you precocious, but when the heat is off, as it was in America–1940, and if you haven't been fatally scarred yet, you return with a bump to your real age. The war, of course, continued with or without me, and I rooted dutifully for the British 8th Army in Africa as it turned the tide at El Alamein and battled cheerily for To-bruk, but my war rooting and my sports rooting became more and more indistinguishable, until, by the dreadful September of 1942, I was turning to the war news as an escape from the sports pages.

But I am still staring at that beaning story. God knows, *PM* didn't give you much to work with. On the very good chance that you've never heard of it, let me just say that it was a minimalist journal of opinion that assumed you'd already read another newspaper and wouldn't be needing any more news today. So reading it was like looking at a series of still lifes and imagining for yourself the cottage in Provence and the peasant who'd put the apple on the table. What had happened, I now knew, went something like this:

Leo Durocher, who would be one of my archetypes, that

is, one of my most thoroughly examined grown-ups, had left the St. Louis Cardinals two years earlier to play shortstop for and eventually manage the Brooklyn Dodgers, leaving, if I know my Leo, a fund of ill will behind him. As a player, Durocher had been limited, extremely limited in fact. All he had was a good pair of hands and a great baseball brain—or maybe it was great hands and a good brain—and an ability to stir things up that is mercifully given to few mortals in any one period—Al Sharpton, Mussolini, Abbie Hoffman, just a few.

Leo must have decided early in life that if he couldn't play *their* game as well as they did, he would make them play his, and the name of his game was Uproar. It was simplicity itself: if you made everyone too mad to know what they were doing, you won. This game must have appealed to Branch Rickey, another of my archetypes who'll make a proper entrance with trumpets later. Rickey was at the time trying to maneuver one of the smallest bankrolls in baseball through the shoals of the depression and past the bigger bankrolls of New York and Chicago, and he needed an edge, any edge. And the edge he settled on was Durocher's game of Uproar, which Rickey's team of hungry country boys was already superbly equipped to play, what with not only the Master himself at short, but such formidable players as "Muscles" (mark him well) Medwick in left, Dizzy and Daffy Dean on the mound, and Pepper Martin on the washboard (the clubhouse played Uproar too). Just to make their point totally clear, the team called itself the "Gashouse Gang," thus buying itself extra ink wherever it went and an aura that hung around the batting cage making the players' every move significant.

The saga of the Gashouse Gang reminds one, in sober retrospect, of one of those Irish uprisings that lasts five minutes and gives birth to a hundred songs. The boys

fought and sang their way to exactly one world championship and a couple of great pennant races, before dying and
spewing the team's remains over the rest of the league.
Dizzy Dean went to the Cubs with a suspect arm, manager
Frankie Frisch went off shaking his head to Pittsburgh, and
Durocher as noted proceeded to Brooklyn, where he an-
gled to acquire, among others, "Muscles" (alias "Ducky")
Medwick, his brawling buddy ("Joe knocks 'em down before the fight even gets interesting," said Dizzy Dean). And
there the two ex-Gashousers could be found riding together in an elevator in Brooklyn in July 1940, exchanging
insults with the Cardinal manager, Billy Southworth, and his
young pitcher Bob Bowman.

It was all there in that San Francisco attic in a one-para-
graph story: the New York of 1940 with all its bustle and
noise and super-bright sunlight, as it had once been per-
ceived by a nine-year-old Britisher. Picture if you will four
men of the period in straw fedoras (I don't see these guys
taking their hats off in an elevator) spitting out challenges
in period pidgen: my guy can lick your guy! Oh yeah? Oh
yeah!

Durocher used to pal around with George Raft in those
days, maybe for drama coaching, so it was probably his
scene all the way. But Medwick also gloried in his toughness, so it's not fair to blame Leo for everything that happened that afternoon. Maybe Bob Bowman was wild and
would have hit Joe anyhow. At any rate, he was certainly too
wild to play the game of Chicken that Durocher was pro-
posing in the elevator. One of his pitches came in tighter
than tight, and Ducky, who always raised his front leg (like
Mel Ott, only less so) before swinging, may have been
caught off balance, and at any rate failed to live up to his
second pseudonym. And for the rest of the season, Ducky
had double vision, and his average plummeted, never fully

to return. Although his eyes would right themselves in time, he was never the same aggressive hitter, and it was hinted in the press and bellowed from opposing dugouts that he might be just a teensy bit gun-shy. So we heard less about his toughness, except as it was subsumed into the general infuriating swagger of Durocher's new team the Dodgers, or Gashouse Gang II.

Medwick's beaning was the kind of chance you took with Durocher: he won pennants for you but he lost them in very much the same way. His game of Uproar was always turning around and biting him, as the above episode shows nicely. Taunting a kid fireballer in those pre–batting helmet days wasn't shrewd, it was crazy, and it suggests why this hyperthyroid big roller was only spottily successful as a manager.

But to say that is to simplify too much and too soon: it is like trying to sum up a Dostoyevski novel in one sentence. Durocher and I would spend a long turbulent life together, but not that afternoon in the attic. All I wanted to hold in my mind as I descended the stairs reluctantly was a picture of Ebbets Field on a hot bright day with that ball park's trademark cheerfulness tucked away for now and the blood high as the two best teams in the league squared away. Then the parry-thrust of called balls and strikes and foul balls slapping back on the screen, or sizzling down the line inches foul, and then oh my God! he isn't moving. The look on Durocher at that moment, the look on Bowman. And then, as if to break the spell, the look of the Dodgers' choleric owner Larry MacPhail as he burst from the stands and challenged the whole Cardinal bench to come out and fight. All this would be part of Dodger lore when I became a fan, and I could see it now as clearly as generations of Greeks must have "seen" Achilles dragging Hector's body around the walls of Troy. The Dodgers lost the 1940 pennant that day, but the Cardinals didn't win it. In September, the Cincinnati Reds, sleeping catcher and all, slipped past both of them as they glared at each other, with maybe the weakest team ever to win a pennant in peacetime.

But that was enough for now. It was already January 1975, and if I held my breath just a little bit longer, we'd have a new season starting with God knew what new stories for the scrapbook. Maybe, for instance, a Red Sox catcher would cause a home run to stay fair by sheer force of will in maybe the greatest World Series game ever played next October.

Forget it. Not even baseball could come up with something as crazy as that.

2

Grandstands and Radios

Summers seem to take so long at the age of ten or so that I now remember the 1941 edition as at least three different summers. In one of them I saw my first ball game. That's all. Then a long time elapsed, and I was *much* older—and I began seeing lots of games, every single Sunday in fact, until I went off to boarding school for the first time. And then, *way* later, and older than time itself by now, listening to the World Series on Father Anthony's radio and wondering how the Yankees could be so lucky.

The filing system in that part of my brain is unbelievably sloppy. When did I start listening to the radio, for instance, and where did we find time to visit Cape Cod? But the first game still sits there shining. The scene of my Baseball Mitzvah was Shibe Park, and aging commuters will remember how the sight of that park brightened the approach to North Philadelphia station. You had only to hop off the train and be in Wonderland (I hopped off myself one day and landed on my nose—you did have to wait until the train stopped). Anyway, it was love at first sight, a love embracing even the light towers and the back of the grandstand. This was going to be a good place. Yes indeed.

In Shibe Park of 1941, kids could scamper in a way that is impossible in any park today. God knows the Philadelphia crowds were manageable; in fact if you went on a weekday you practically had the place to yourself, and could take home all the foul balls you could carry. But even a small crowd produces a certain kind of pleasurable baseball hum punctuated by gasps, and this is your entrance music as you race behind the ramps, looking through the slits and trying to pick the strip of field you want to overlook. Outside of a few box seats on the ground floor, everything was up for grabs back then and if you had the energy you could watch every inning from a different angle. But we settled on a spot in back of first, and stepped into the appropriate tunnel, the birth canal, and into the most beautiful sight I'd ever seen: it would be another year or two before I recognized beauty in real scenery, or even understood the concept "beauty," but I already knew this was beautiful.

Shibe Park was totally green. Besides the greenest grass ever seen anywhere, it had green seats and olive-green walls, unadulterated by advertising. The color scheme was in fact broken only by crisp white numbers, 331 in right, 334 in left, and 468 in dead center. Perfect. Connie Mack, the venerable owner-manager of the Philadelphia A's who *was* baseball in Philadelphia, was funny about money. He sold all his great players for cash, but he wouldn't take advertising on his walls—although it's just possible that he wasn't offered any, his teams were so bad.

But I didn't know that. All I can say is, the walls looked perfect to me. Having hacked around the schoolyard with a small rubber ball and schoolmates who complicated life by trying to catch this ball with baseball gloves (try it some time), I was at the stage of being amazed that the players here didn't drop the ball in infield practice or shake uncontrollably as those stratospheric fly balls descended on them.

The gods of baseball tested me sternly that day by laying on two of the worst teams in baseball, the A's and the St. Louis Browns, both of which have since gone mercifully out of existence, but better teams would have been wasted. It takes one game just to enjoy the park—the strange shape of the golden infield dirt (to this day, I look for baseball diamonds first when I fly over a new city) and the well-tended, grandly unnecessary strip between the mound and the plate that told you this was a big-league park which did things in a big-league way.

There was a fence in right field at Shibe as there would be at Ebbets, while the bleachers were in left, and that was as it should be. Just as the first house you live in is in some sense the model for all houses later, so I still judge ballparks on a scale of how closely they approximate Shibe Park, Wrigley Field coming perhaps closest except for that strange fungus on the walls, and Fenway Park coming close, too, except that it's built the wrong way around. Tiger Stadium looks fine in left but then repeats itself in right. Too bad. Yankee Stadium is something else, a law unto itself. It has earned the right to look any way it pleases and I wouldn't change a seat of it. Forget most of the rest.

The game that day also showed me the perfection of the measurements at Shibe. Wally Moses clipped a home run to right, just the right length, while "Indian" Bob Johnson

pounded one to left—the verbs are not just elegant variations, but descriptions of their styles of hitting. Owing to
the effects of foreshortening, balls hit away from you seem
to be battling the elements, so I would have to sit in back
of third to appreciate Johnson's future home runs to the
full. He had the measure of the home-park left-field fence
the way Ralph Kiner would in Pittsburgh, and he drilled
balls into the seats with the accuracy of Jack Nicklaus hitting
greens with an eight-iron—all this while enduring the Indian war whoops that attended his every move (I thought
the crowd had gone nuts the first time I saw them flapping
their hands against their mouths and shouting "whooo").

Baseball has it in common with the movies that even if
the story is a dog, there is always something to catch your
interest—a piece of camera work, a curious field place-
ment: William McGeehan once wrote a whole piece describing the shock that ran through the baseball world
when the Pittsburgh manager failed to play the infield "in"
in a World Series game. There is always *something* going
on, and for a newcomer there was everything—the way the
players tossed their gloves over their shoulders, as they did
in those days, after the third out, or flipped their sunglasses
down as they drifted magnetically toward fly balls. My God,
this was heaven—another concept I hadn't fully understood. I loved this game, and wanted to see it every day for
the rest of my life. And everyone around me seemed to feel
the same way, it was like a revivalist meeting—though all
that seemed to be reviving at that moment were the Philadelphia A's.

The crowd at ball games always starts off coiled tight, and
the first foul ball almost sends it into hysterics. But eventually it needs a good game if it is to maintain this pitch and
not go home feeling mysteriously deflated. I doubt if I
would ever have come down from my high that day, but I'll

never know for sure, because the game, from an Athletic point of view, which had so far barked like a dog and wagged its tail like a dog and waddled like a turkey for good measure, suddenly rallied for the better. The A's, who had been acting out their usual version of the death scene from *Camille,* suddenly came to life and began pounding and chipping their way back to win 10–8—a score that had old-timers remembering eleven years back (eleven years!—these must be very old people) to the greatest comeback in World Series history and babble-babble—it wouldn't be till next summer (about three weeks from now) that I would know what they were talking about, after which I would know a ridiculous amount about it. The residents of Torresdale, Pennsylvania, averaged about eighty-three years old apiece by my estimate, so I had to learn about the past as quickly as possible in order to talk to these people at all, and my baseball face began life turned backwards.

It is an affliction of rookie fans—and of New York fans for the rest of their lives—to take each individual game much too seriously (Durocher and Billy Martin were the perfect New York managers, both of them having a sense of proportion out of El Greco: normal people would burn out at that skewed intensity). As I floated out of Shibe Park that day I knew for sure that I had seen not only one of the greatest games of all time, but one of the greatest teams. The Athletics' problems, if they had ever had any, were definitely behind them now. This game had turned the tide, the team had begun to hit, and the next 120 or so would be a cakewalk.

The 1941 team was, oddly enough, just good enough to sustain such illusions (or could it be that my memory still hasn't grown up?). Besides Johnson and Moses, who were obviously the best around, we had Dick Siebert (.334 that year) at first and Sam Chapman (.322) in center. Frankie

Hayes had to be the best catcher in the league—and who knew from pitching in those days? They had a few pitchers in the National League, I believe, and Bobby Feller in this one, but half of the AL teams had no-name pitching staffs, and our no-names were probably at least as good as theirs were. In fact we even had a certified Yankee killer: Johnny Babich, who'd gotten away from their farm system, had beaten the Yankees five times last year in revenge. He never made a move without this fact being announced—and that was better than anyone on the Red Sox could have done. The Red Sox, indeed, seemed to have practically dispensed with pitching altogether, as well you might if you had Dom DiMaggio, Ted Williams, Jim Tabor, Joe Cronin, Jimmy Foxx, and Bobby Doerr batting for you, and they seemed none the worse for it, finishing second or third every year without it.

Precocious kids always get at least one important thing wrong. The National League was known as a pitchers' league in the thirties and the American League as a hitters' league and these descriptions became absolutes to me. And since the American League always won the World Series and the All-Star Game, what was a guy to think? I hadn't yet absorbed the fact that the Yankees usually won the American League pennant by about 20 games—Roy Stockton, the St. Louis writer, used to refer to the league as "Snow White and the Seven Dwarfs." Nor, obviously, did I grasp that a 3.80 earned run average beats a 4.50, especially if you have only a 5.70, a 7.20, and a kid just up from Winston-Salem in the bull pen, or that Connie Mack, aged 1,000 by now, didn't know pitching from Shinola any more.

Old Mr. Mack was my other memory of that day. All one could usually catch of him from the grandstand was the lower half of a black or gray suit and a waving scorecard, with which he allegedly did all his managing—and that's all

I *ever* saw of him the dozens of other times I went to Shibe
Park. Yet he was as much of a presence as any manager I've
ever seen the whole of, including Lippy himself.

My ignorance did receive a powerful kick in the slats that
July, when not a single Athletic was chosen to the 1941 All-
Star team. This was impossible, wasn't it? It must be another
typo, like the Bears score last winter. An American League
team without Bob Johnson and Wally Moses? Hey. You learn
early in life that Philadelphia is a bit of a joke, but we're
talking here about a serious insult. I expected rioting in the
streets.

I was affronted, but I learned. It seems fair to say that
Arky Vaughan's two home runs in the All-Star Game and
Ted Williams's game-winning home run introduced me to
the rest of baseball—which up to then had consisted entirely of Joe DiMaggio's burgeoning hitting streak. There
were a *lot* of good players out there, were there not? The
newsreels that summer majored in frames of Williams
prancing exultantly around the bases after his hit, acting the
way I felt. Baseball is a *kick,* a trip to the moon, and Williams
was man enough to admit it. So. Winter was the Bears,
grinding it out. Summer was the Kid, as they sometimes
called him, dancing and whooping in the lights of the Polo
Grounds, happy enough to burst. Football was work, like
plowing snow; baseball was play. An easy call.

I returned to the season proper immensely enriched by
this one-night caper. Joe DiMaggio's streak had so far tran-
scended baseball, it belonged to the whole world, and even
old ladies who didn't know which way the label should face
when you hit the ball knew all about the Yankee Clipper.
Life and even baseball seemed to stop as Joe swept regally
past Tris Speaker and Wee Willie Keeler—incidentally con-

firming my impression that batting in the American League was pretty much target practice that year. I did learn the names of a lot of pitchers, but strictly as whipping boys and milestones, and I noted that it took two of them, Al Milner and Jim Bagby, plus a great third baseman in Ken Keltner, finally to bring the Clipper to ground, after which he went on another 12-game tear just for the hell of it. (I only recently learned that early on in *the* streak, DiMaggio got a suspect hit off Keltner's glove; I don't know why, but that eases my mind quite a bit.)

But the All-Star Game showed me that there was more to baseball than DiMaggio, and maybe even another league than the American. Just as Joe began gracefully to recede from view, my first real pennant race came roaring down the track, and it wasn't where I'd been looking at all, but in the National League. The Brooklyn Dodgers had caught the nation's fancy—or perhaps been crammed down the nation's craw by the New York writers—to the point where they had begun to cross the line out of baseball and into pop culture as DiMaggio had. Comedians made jokes about them, Red Skelton would even make a movie about them, and when America finally joined the war, they would be perfectly positioned for insertion into war-movie dialogue. The Dodgers *created* William Bendix as the eternal serviceman from Flatbush or Canarsie forever inquiring after his beloved Bums as the smoke clears in Iwo Jima and Okinawa, and he returned the compliment with all the free advertising a business could use.

America's team. Were they really that? Probably as much so as anyone has been since. Strangers need something to talk about as the World Series approaches each year, and a Durocher team, whatever else might be said about it, always gave you plenty to talk about, even if it was only about Leo himself. As Durocher stormed around the league that August, brandishing his team like a revolver, people were forced to ask themselves where they stood concerning this man—was he a real American character, or a deplorable sign of the times? Was he a good old baseball boy in the style of John McGraw or a thug in the style of John Dillinger?

Whatever he was, he suited a ten-year-old fine. I had never met a truly coarse or brutal adult up close, so I guess I thought it was all an act, and I felt free to admire him as I admired Long John Silver in Treasure Island and other make-believe villains. Seeing him on television in later years, I had trouble remembering why anyone took him so seriously—there didn't seem to be that much to him any more. But the years can shrink certain things beyond recognition, and the passage of time could only subtract from a guy like Leo. Taking away his manic energy was like removing the battery from a complicated toy: you could hardly even guess what it was *for.*

Indeed, by the late sixties, when he served his last stint with the Cubs, Durocher hardly seemed able to remember himself; by then he was a rather sour parody of his old self, annoying people without charming them or otherwise winning them over. But in 1941, he was just hitting his prime, hypnotizing and galvanizing his players until they seemed like extensions of himself, and even taking over for a few masterly games at short when his ace rookie Pee Wee Reese came down with the jitters. (In the other league, Frank Crosetti spelled young Phil Rizzuto very briefly for the same reason. Later Rizzuto would sign an article in the *Saturday Evening Post,* describing how the sight of George Case, the fastest Senator in history, racing to first froze him. If they were all going to run like that, he didn't belong here.)

"Are you a Dodger fan?" my father asked jovially one early day in September, and although I remember that we were coming out of church, and I even remember what the weather was like (delightful), I can't for the life of me summon up what I answered him. The problem was that on the one hand, I knew that *all* little boys liked the Dodgers, it was inexpressibly corny; but on the other hand you had the curious fact that WOR Radio reached Torresdale, and I had taken to listening to Red Barber's broadcasts of Dodger games and had been seduced, even as larger men than I had, by that great man's welcome-to-Florida style. So I was not being just another trendy little boy about this.

"Raht now, the bases are F.O.B.—fulluv Brooklyns," he would purr. "Whitlow Wyatt [I can still hear that one. *Beautiful.*] seems to be sittin' in the cat-bird seat, ma friends." Around that time, James Thurber wrote a story in which those phrases are grounds for murder, and within a few years I would have understood this perfectly. By then I had grown to loathe not only the smarmy little phrases but the syrup they came in—and then would grow in my old age to love them again. "Whit-low Wahtt." Hell, yes. By now, I even miss the nerve-racking *tick-tick* (pause) *tick* of the telegraph machine from which Barber wove half of his broadcast. "The flags are barely rifflin' today in Crosley, ma friends [*tick*] which means theah's prob'ly just the merest hint of a breeze blowin' off the Ohio Rivuh—[*tick, tick*]—meanwahl, Frank McCormick adjusts the bill of his cap and Kubby Higbe looks in long and slow for the sign [*tick,* pause]—whoops [*long* pause, and *tickety-tick, tick*] he *jest* missed with that one, a fastball hah inside—you know how ol' Kubby lo–oves that pitch" (Barber knows anyway and gives Kirby Higbe about 70 of them a game).

And so on through the drowsy afternoon. It was only, as usual, later that I realized that the old Redhead used to spin most of this flapdoodle out of his head, embroidering it around the bare words that came off his tickertape. "Batter, McCormick. Ball one." "Mah, that was a venomous glare the

Reds slugger jest shot back at the mound. It looks like we've got a regl'r barney brewin' here, folks, between Messrs. Higbe and McCormick."

At the time, I guess I thought that Barber probably kept some kind of ticking machine in his booth as a sound effect to simulate excitement, the way Walter Winchell would later. Since the radio audience was straining to see the game itself through the mesh in the set, every little bit helped.

Anyway, it was all part of the excitement as the 1941 pennant-race express picked up steam with me and thousands of others hanging from the sides. But how to explain that to my cricket-loving, baseball-condescending Aussie father? How also to explain that I really *knew* baseball now, and wasn't some fair-weather pipsqueak along for the ride?

Sometime that July, I had discovered I could get to Shibe Park by myself. It was a trek by any standards—a long walk, a trolley ride, a subway-cum-El ride, and a long walk, and then the whole thing in reverse to come home—but that was a detail. You simply adjusted your screen each time and let the daydreams roll until you got there. With a double-header in front of me, or the memories of one in back of me, I could have walked to Mecca through burning sand. The only problem was money, and my mother took care of that: good woman though she was, she also knew the value of having a rabid coolie in the family who would kill for the price of a hot dog, and she set me to work mowing the lawn and hoeing our vestigial victory garden (the Americans weren't at war yet, and we had a jump on them) until I'd accumulated enough scratch to start another pilgrimage.

Our lawn was a big one, and it absorbed an awful lot of daydreaming. "Ted Williams—I'm going to see Ted Williams" could see you all the way through from Monday. But what did you do when the White Sox were coming to town? "I'm going to see Mike Kreevich" didn't hold up for half an

hour. "Myril Hoag, Joe Kuhel, Mike Tresh, Don Kolloway"
—there wasn't, as they say, a single stopper on the whole
squad. Maybe Ted Lyons would pitch, *he* was famous. "The
best pitcher who's never been in a World Series" would be
better than nothing, I supposed. But then again you learn
early that one pitcher is much like another from behind
first or third. And after you're through admiring their motions, which aren't always that distinctive anyway, the only
way you can tell they're great is that no one seems able to
hit them—and who wants that?

So maybe Lyons wouldn't pitch and maybe, oh Lord grant
me this one wish and I'll leave you alone forever, the A's
would hit. (After their outburst against the Browns that day,
they'd subsided a bit.) Or maybe there'd be a triple play or
a tape-measure home run. And what did I know about Joe
Kuhel anyway? I looked him up in my new *Who's Who*
magazine, and he'd had a pretty interesting career. Washington, World Series (Washington?)—a lot of so-so stuff. So
inflate! Make him important. And hey, it's *baseball*—big-
league baseball. Which meant, if all else failed, that you at
least got to see the most elegant practice sessions before
the game to be found in any sport, including music.

Offhand, I can't think of any other sport, except maybe
billiards, where the practice sessions are worth the price of
admission. With golf, the rehearsing pro works on one
stroke at a time until he has it down, and the audience out,
cold; with tennis, the players either play it or they don't—
there is no in-between way of doing it that's worth looking
at for more than a minute or so; with football you need
another team in front of you; and even with basketball,
baseball's closest rival, the practicers seem to revert in no
time to the bounce-bounce-shoot of the playground, and
you're reminded annoyingly of the sport's limitations.

In contrast, baseball warm-ups express the essence of

47

their sport almost more satisfyingly than the game itself does. At the center of the canvas, you'll see a bunch of guys lounging around the batting cage forming one of those immemorial American tableaux of "hanging out"—around a pool room, around a cracker barrel—ribbing and riding one another inaudibly and talking cryptic body language to the kid in the stands—until one of them breaks off the conversation and darts into the cage like a cat to grab a quick swing out of turn, as if one batting practice cut were the world's most coveted privilege. Next, the guy who's *supposed* to be hitting barges in and chases the interloper out with his bat while the latter covers his ass in feigned terror and hops out of range—and you realize that at least some of these guys are having almost as much fun out there as you would be.

And that isn't the half of it. Out in left field there's another fellow working on catching fly balls behind his back (he just bobs his head at the last minute, and *voilà*). This is art for art's sake, because he'll never be able to use his trick in a game and nobody's watching him now, except you. Meanwhile further behind his back a couple of pitchers are matching strides and talking philosophy ("Boy, what a night"), as they plow through their obligatory legwork.

In front of the home-team dugout, some guys are playing a little pepper, which is the absolute core and nub of baseball practice. In case you've missed it, which is possible these days, a game of pepper consists of three or so fielders taking turns either tossing the ball to a nearby batter who bunts it back smartly, or flipping it sideways to each other or conceivably juggling it themselves for a moment—behind the back, through the legs, whatever. The ball is constantly in motion one way or another, with the batter varying the tempo and taxing the fielders' reflexes with popups or quasi line drives—and then, when it's time to stop, sometimes doing all this in full retreat until he backs all the way into the dugout and disappears.

Pepper could almost be a nursery game, and as played by me and my friends at school in the next few years, it surely was. But seeing things done right is what ballparks are for, and a game of pepper at the big-league level is as pretty a sight as Luther Lassiter or some other pool pro showing off trick shots: it loosens up the spectators almost as much as the players and reminds them, amid the artificial grimness of the Season or the Tournament, of what games are all about.

As with any three-ring circus, you can go crazy deciding what to look at during batting practice. Paul Waner practicing his throws—or possibly sobering up (Waner had a beautiful arm and a prodigious thirst, so it could go either way); a star pitcher taking a few grounders at shortstop and almost getting killed by a stray fungo; or maybe the visiting team emerging piecemeal from the dugout and throwing on the sidelines—that's Roy Weatherly all right, but what is he trying to throw, a knuckleball?

It would take a painter with the peripheral vision of Brueghel to do justice to all these craftsmen working away simultaneously at their own specialties and each other's, with one team moving onto the field and the other retreating in an unbroken flow, batting practice for two and fielding practice for two being timed to the very minute—and everywhere baseballs, *hard*balls, flying around their heads, a thousand potential concussions effortlessly avoided (one stray ball was always enough to conk one kid in the games I played in, and fetch a call from his mother, if not the family lawyer).

I have never understood fans who pass up this feast of plenty to settle for a mere nine-man, nine-inning game— let alone those fans on the West Coast who seem to favor the five-inning game (Los Angeles attendance records would look a lot scrawnier if they had to be based on "innings attended"). You can beat the traffic just as easily by arriving at dawn for afternoon games and leaving after they kick you out. Or you could in those days. Shibe Park seemed in fact so casual and ill-attended that you felt as if you could probably have locked up after the game and seen your*self* out for all it cared.

Your eyes wander now around the field pausing and resting at the sideshows but returning always to the hub of the picture, the batting cage, because that is where you get to see what's on today's menu. Someday, it might be a Natural like young Eddie Mathews, whom even the other players leave their private worlds to watch, or the kid with the wrists, Hank Aaron. But today you have to settle for the likes of Luke Appling, the peerless foul-ball hitter and hypochondriac, who looks less like a ballplayer than anyone you've ever seen but at least you've heard of him, and Moose Solters, who maybe reaches the seats a couple of times—fortunately everyone tends to look good in batting practice, so you simply pick a guy you'd like to look like yourself someday, or whose swing would be fun to imitate: who *knows* why you pick your favorites?

As I say, they all look their best against puff-ball pitching, and by game time I knew for sure I would be watching yet another battle of Titans, even if the prize only *is* seventh place.

Above all the various Titans that summer reigned the gods, Jupiter and Apollo, the yin and the yang, the classical DiMaggio and the romantic Williams, and my excitement almost tipped over into apoplexy when the Red Sox rolled into Philadelphia in August, riding twenty-five different cabs even then. (The Red Sox personality problem has been one of the givens of baseball for all of my conscious life, along with rumors that "this year it's different." Don't you believe them. If you trade Babe Ruth, you're lucky to get off with a sentence of eternity.)

Ted Williams would hang around long enough to live through several phases, like Picasso. But that year, he was strictly the young poet from the outback and a stranger to men's rules. He dressed, so far as the laws of baseball allowed, like a premature hippie, with his pants drooping around his ankles and his shirt ever on the verge of popping out, and he didn't so much play left field as "hang out" in the area, looking bored and waiting for the real action to start, namely for himself to hit.

I don't suppose in baseball history that any player of however peculiar size or shape has ever been easier to spot in the field than Williams, if only because he was the only one out there who didn't wait for the next pitch with his hands on his knees or his body crouched, but stood, at least when I first saw him, draped languidly like one of the aesthetes in Gilbert and Sullivan's *Patience*. In later phases, and after a stiff stint in the military, his fielding would sharpen out of sight, and his pants would rise to the base of his shins. But right now he was still "the Kid" thumbing his nose at Boston, at neckties, at anything that threatened for one moment to fence him in: James Dean in spikes and before his time.

But the Kid's clothes and manners were just the accoutrements of rebellion, the props and flourishes: the real breakthrough, and the poetry, was in the hitting. I had already read in my bible (a magazine called simply *Baseball* that I kept by my bed in case I died during the night) of how Williams could start his swing so late that Birdie Tebbetts the catcher swore that the swooping bat plucked the ball out of his mitt, and I had seen pictures of the pretzels he formed with his follow-through (any pictures you see of these are pre-war). There was something wrong with this picture. Even at that age I knew my catechism inside out, and I knew that the guys who hit .400, as Williams was doing right now, were "contact" hitters who just met the ball: they definitely did not turn into pretzels.

If my older self can horn in for a moment, before he goes nuts listening to these embryonic opinions (non–baseball fans can take a breather here while the rest of you assume your batting stances)—dogma was, as it turns out, only half right about this. Sluggers do lose points from having to commit themselves so soon, but they gain them back quickly when they connect, for the simple reason that a hard-hit ball has a much better chance in life than a soft one. Contact hitters really have to scratch for a living, beating out grounders and Baltimore chops and watching their best shots flagged down with mechanical certainty, while louts like Harmon Killebrew can strike out all afternoon and still go 1 for 4 on a stray bouncer up the middle. So .400 hitters have to hit the ball *pretty* hard, like, say, Stan Musial or George Brett—or else (quaint exception) be as left-handed as they but stroke the ball to left, like Wade Boggs or Rod Carew. What you don't have to do, and in fact would probably have to be crazy to *try* to do, would be to swing as hard as Ted Williams.

So at whatever age you watched him, he was a miracle, and when he took his cuts in the cage that day, you knew you were seeing something special. People were taking note of this to describe when they got home, or to their bored grandchildren, or to strangers yet unborn in saloons yet unopened. "I saw Williams the year he hit .400. He . . ." Well, what? His feet were slightly closer and his stride longer than they would be by the time he got through with his tinkering and quit baseball in 1960, but he squirmed as much as ever, as if his suit were filled with flea powder, before coming to a statuesque halt, and he lashed the ball harder than any man has ever done before or since, including himself. After the war, he would pack a little extra weight through the chest and legs, and could plow the extra energy into control; savage iron control of the kind that breaks bats in your hands, but back then he was *skinny* out of sight, and letting it all hang out.

Yet for all that, his hitting was almost lost in the shuffle that day. Somebody must have forgotten to tell the Red Sox that batting practice was over and they just kept batting around and around, and I can't remember exactly who did what, but I'm pretty sure that Tabor hit a couple out, and Cronin hit at least one, and Doerr probably—and above all, I had a new hero, as one so often did by the end of those long days. Jimmy Foxx hit two shots into the light towers in left which if they'd been allowed to go any further would probably have landed someplace in the Susquehanna River, after orbiting the globe. Now *there* was a man who hit the ball hard—and for good averages too. Standing underneath these space probes, Indian Bob Johnson assumed once and for all his proper size—that of a very good mortal, a Tommy Henrich plus, but no god, not even a little one.

Trying to rate Jimmy Foxx today, one finds oneself staring across the Great Divide, the slider, which lies between the extravagant hitting statistics of the thirties and the pinch-penny ones of today. Before this humiliating little pitch came along, it was possible to let out all the slack in your swing without getting egg on your face too often. There were only two real pitches to worry about, the curve and the fastball (the few change-up pitches of the era were a joke—you could spot them coming from the stands), and both of the big two declared themselves early to big-league eyes like Foxx's, which could lay their plans accordingly. The slider or "nickel curve," with its slight extra speed and last-second break, changed all that for good. With the slider, you could only hope that something would go wrong with it—that it would break too soon or too late and, either way, "hang" for a second. Since it looks like a fastball and acts like a curve, it's hard to plan ahead and crank up for it the old way and games today are analyzed much more than they used to be in terms of pitchers' mistakes, rather than hitters' achievements.

So where does that leave someone like Foxx? Remember, he was one of the Fab 5 whom Carl Hubbell struck out in a row in the 1934 All-Star Game with low screwballs in what might be considered a dazzling preview, like a scene briefly lit by lightning, of the modern era—if one new pitch could flummox five of the greatest so easily, why not another new pitch? Why not two or three others?

Some pre-war hitters, notably Williams and Stan Musial, made the cut and crossed the divide with ease; others, surprisingly including DiMaggio, did not. And perhaps Joe's post-war stats, which a lesser man would have been glad to claim but which were spit-backs for him, are as good a guide as we have to how the right-handed sluggers of the thirties would have made out against a pitch that was put on earth expressly to make life a living torment for people like them. Hank Greenberg, who was probably about to fade anyway, faded faster than anyone could possibly have expected. Joe Medwick, Frank McCormick—none of them did anything much, certainly nothing to compare with the best years of Johnny Mize, their left-handed contemporary, for whom the right-handed slider broke obligingly in and not out. Nothing makes you feel your age like embarrassment: in no time your back and feet hurt, and the distance from home and back stretches before you like the Boston Marathon. Even your ideas feel out of date.

But to be fair, we have to imagine these men starting over again in the new world like Ralph Kiner, not straining their pre-war eyes to catch up with it. Ted Williams, who is a careful man with a compliment, has called Jimmy Foxx the second best player he ever saw, so it's hard to believe that he and the first best too (DiMaggio, who else?) wouldn't have found their feet in the new world, staying behind the pitch a little longer, like Kiner, and settling for lower averages and just a little less power. Perhaps the closest post-war counterpart to Foxx would be Mickey Mantle, the right-handed version, at least. Mantle, as I recall, had a slightly more compact swing, and he abstained from Jimmy's death or glory follow-through, in the interests of getting to first like a speeding bullet (unlike most righty sluggers, he didn't hit into many double plays in his right-handed incarnation), but the total effect was startlingly alike, such that I thought old Double X had come around again the first time I saw Mickey swing.

Mantle even resembled Foxx in his conviviality (as it was politely called then) and his rapid descent from the heights: both men admitted to having trouble sighting the ball sometime in their mid-thirties. But unlike the Mick, Jimmy kept right on descending from there, fetching up in a rooming house down South from which the Detroit Tigers tried poignantly to rescue him by making him a hitting coach, only to watch him descend again. Reading this a few years later, I felt the way kids presumably do when they find their old man passed out drunk on the porch. This was my hero, and it was a sad thing. But I was lucky to catch him just before the Fall. A year after I first saw him, he was traded to the National League where a friend of a friend who was trying out for the Phillies reported that he found Foxx and his old buddy Jim Tabor careening off the walls of their hotel room, too drunk to stand up. *Requiescant* to both of them.

But real life and its messes were still a million miles away that endless afternoon of the thousand hits. I had no idea what these guys did after work; in fact I couldn't even imagine them in regular suits. I had read in my *Baseball* magazine that some of them were champion hotel lobby sitters, seeing who could stare at the potted plants longest, and that Rogers Hornsby and Ted Williams alike never went to the movies because the flickering screen might hurt their eyes. The article didn't say anything about careening off walls.

Although Williams did manage to insert one vintage home run into the bacchanalia of hitting, what he demonstrated most that day was his second greatest gift, namely, drawing walks. There was no point to it, nobody needed him on base, and with that lineup, no one was sure as heck trying to pitch around him. It was just that Ted never allowed his concentration so much as an afternoon off. All in all, he got only 185 hits that year, which is almost impossibly little for a .400 hitter, but he also picked up 175 walks, which is impossibly much, and almost all of them, to judge from my experience of Williams over the years, were carefully worked out, and frowned over to the nearest half inch.

One other insight I picked up that afternoon was the real reason Williams would put his .400 average at risk by staying in the lineup the last day of the season even after the .400 was secure. It was simple. He was batting against the Athletics.

Speaking of whom, it appeared that their cakewalk to the pennant, or even seventh place, had run into certain difficulties, and that even a ten-year-old might consider just giving up on them for this year (next year, watch out; the illusion that your team is just a year away is, of course, what makes the whole thing work). The Dodger games which had so far just been ticking along, not making much sense, suddenly started to take shape, so that took care of the competitive side of things. Shibe Park was for exhibitions, as in "The Detroit Tigers and Barney McCosky will be giving an exhibition this Sunday [I saw Charlie Gehringer get one of his last hits, a tactful line drive over second], and the Sunday after that, the Cleveland Indians will be showing, featuring Hal Trosky and young Lou Boudreau and the distinguished soloist (if you're very lucky) Maestro Robert Feller himself."

The Saturday night before Lord DiMaggio blew in was apoplexy time again. The weather all day had been sultry and I remember placing my chair by the window so I could watch and listen to it all night, or as long as I could stand. The thick, ominous screens they used to put on windows back then tended to make any weather look pretty bad, and the indeterminate rustling of a summer night might have meant anything, so it was an anxious, bug-eyed vigil, what with DiMaggio at stake: but my chief memory of it does not concern the Clipper but a jingle I'd invented and couldn't get out of my head in honor of the early drafting of Hank Greenberg into the U.S. Armed Forces and sung to the tune of the current hit song "Somebody Else is Taking your Place." My version went "Somebody else is taking your place/somebody else is playing first base," and it haunts me still.

The weather, with its alternating signs of a perfect day and a horrible one, continued to play games with me all through Sunday, leaving me strung out and vexed out of my mind. First off it was announced that the great DiMaggio would not be playing today, which took the wind out of me completely—but okay, that still left some pretty good boys: Keller, Gordon, Dickey (He's been scratched too? cheezt, how can they do this to me?), okay, Henrich, Rolfe, I'll take whatever you've got. They're still the New York Yankees, they still had the aura in their spruce, blue-looking road uniforms. Let's just get going before anybody else gets sick around here.

But it was one of those nightmare cat-and-mouse games all the way, threatening at first not to start at all, and then repeating its threats every half inning, as we crept inexorably past the four-and-a-half-inning mark that erased the value of our rain checks, before quitting on us completely after seven. In the meantime I had seen a home run by Twinkletoes Selkirk and another by Joe Gordon (my new hero *du jour*), and years later, when I had discovered cricket and encountered some *real* rain delays, I might have considered this a pretty good day's play. But that was then and this was now, and I left the park feeling sourer than I would have thought possible in that sublime setting.

On the way out, the public address system changed all that for the briefest of moments by informing us that our rain checks would be honored the next time the Yankees came to town and hey, maybe DiMaggio would be feeling better. But the reprieve only made things worse, because then he named the dates, and I knew the worst. We were going to be away in Wildwood, New Jersey, whatever that was, for all those days, and I'd miss DiMaggio *again*. Helplessly I reached for swear words that weren't there yet: *gee-willikers* and *gosh-darn* were of no help. The strangers all around me seemed to be taking all this in stride, though it was hard to tell from where I stood (I was a regular shrimp), and in the bustle of an emptying ballpark there was no one to talk to anyway.

For the whole long journey home in the jiggling light of

the trolley, I nursed the small wild hope, which was probably worse than despair itself, that I could talk my parents into changing their plans. And maybe for a few moments after I got home I may have thought I had: my mother had a tendency to dither over plans ("*Perhaps* we could do this instead of that, or—I don't know, there's a lot to be said for that instead of this—I'll talk to your father about it") and she hated to disappoint any of us. But if any of this happened, and I remember it so clearly that it almost must have, I was in for another bitter lesson regarding the inexorability of adult plans, upon which my father had a firmer grip than my mother. Wildwood, New Jersey, was fixed in the stars, and my rain check was worthless again.

Wildwood was just the first symptom of a problem that would dog me for several years to come. *Everything* that came up in the summer was a nuisance if it did not relate directly to baseball. Wildwood would finally ingratiate itself to me by introducing me to my first batting cage, with an Iron Mike flipping pitches a few feet for customers to whale into a sack (it takes so little to please). But the weekend of the Yankee series was strictly days of bitterness, days of rue, and I couldn't begin to enjoy this miserable place until they were out of the way. After that, I found a kid from St. Louis who talked incessantly about Johnny Mize (my knowledge of American cities so far was strictly confined to who played there) and together we discovered a vacant lot where we could play catch while we prattled. Whatever complacent mothers may think, it is impossible to play anything remotely resembling baseball in the sand, so I turned my back on the comely beaches of Wildwood and spent my time looking for the scruffiest bits of real estate in town with enough space to swing a bat in. It is possible that nobody has ever gotten less out of a summer resort.

That year, anyway. The next year, I would meet a twelve-year-old girl from Germantown, Pennsylvania, whose company I inexplicably enjoyed, causing my mind to stray from baseball for minutes at a time (Father Doubleday, forgive me).

Anyway, there's no excuse for its wandering now as I write this. Next year, I would finally see Joe DiMaggio, and he would even hit a home run for me, the way Ruth and Gehrig used to hit them for little kids in hospitals except that he was so good he didn't have to be asked. But my 1941 ballpark business was pretty much wrapped up by the time I left Wildwood, leaving me free to concentrate on radio baseball, which was beginning to heat up frantically. In Wildwood, I picked up a magazine devoted entirely to the Dodgers, and my faith was cemented solid. There was a picture of Dolph Camilli holding five baseballs in one hand (I could barely hold one), and a feature on the two Harold R's, "Pee Wee" Reese and "Pistol Pete" Reiser, but the most graphic for me was a short take on pennant-race fever, because it showed these guys well and truly out of uniform, playing cards on trains and pacing hotel rooms, unable to sleep in the heat. Dolph Camilli described sneaking out of his room to eat breakfast at dawn, so he could get the new day started and begin thinking about the next game instead of brooding about yesterday's, the one with the bad hop in the tenth. And finding what? That half the team had beaten him to it? Something like that.

. These were my guys now, and I came panting down the stretch with them—or at least I fully intended to, until at the last minute the radio was turned off with a snap and I was put on the train for my new school where, to my dismay, the kids didn't seem to give much of a damn about baseball, which they considered a game for old farts—*football* was the real American game, boy, and before I knew it I was jiggling around in outsized shoulder pads and pining for my old friend, the radio, a grandfather-sized affair that dominated our living room like an altar. I didn't miss home, I missed baseball.

It came as a shock, the kind that makes you holler out loud, that this so-called national pastime seemed, once you left the big-league cities and certain pockets of enlightenment elsewhere, to be a rather small and cranky cult sport followed by a few lonely souls of the sort who operate ham radios. To boys who had only seen the cow-pasture version, it seemed a hopelessly horse-and-buggy game without chrome or tailfins, or any trace of the twentieth century: it was manifestly too slow, nobody wanted to play catcher, and only the good guys had any fun; it was also a game that could humiliate you unforgivably, isolating you for a moment in space and time as an "easy" pop fly hurtled venomously toward you or a game-winning grounder skittered between your legs.

The fields we played on had no fences and the ball could roll forever as some poor wretch panted over field and farm with the shouts of the base runners growing fainter in his ears. As he reaches down, cursing baseball with every wheezing breath in his body, the ball skips out of his hand. And then again, as the last run scores and the crowd gives a final burp of joy. He is too furious to pick up *anything* by now, even if it had glue on it. Finally he calms down enough to get a handle and heaves the ball into the woods. Or tries to. But we might as well leave him at this point. He will never be a baseball fan.

Occasionally, I would get a chance to slip away to Father Anthony's room where the two of us would huddle like early Christians listening to a few stolen innings of baseball as my philistine schoolmates grunted through the motions of football outside.

Father Anthony was a true believer too, and like all such

he had a bee in his bonnet. He had obtained from Gabby Hartnett, the great Cubs catcher, the names of baseball's most prominent anti-Catholics, including the Hall of Famers Tris Speaker and "Columbia" Eddie Collins, the holier or at least whiter than thou White Sox second baseman on the Chicago team whose socks had turned black when it threw the World Series in 1919. Although nobody liked the fixers on that team, nobody seemed to like Eddie either, who was obviously a prig—and Father Anthony had the proof.

That good man's findings on the religious issue certainly offered a new dimension to the game: those were real people out there all right with real human weaknesses—but who needed that? I decided. There were enough real people outside of baseball already, and I find I had willfully forgotten all about Father Anthony's names until just this minute, when the man himself came back to my mind, wart (he only had one, if that) and all. Father Anthony was, in fact, my patron that year who kept me from the harm a little English kid was due for in a school full of Irish-Americans; he was the one priest it was good to be a friend of (with the rest, you were just a teacher's pet), and to this day, I have never met a kinder or more charming man. Unfortunately he was transferred to Newark before the year was over, and I got my lumps after all.

3

Pain in Toyland

The Dodgers' clinching of the pennant in 1941 filled me
with the kind of elation that one allegedly gets just before
an epileptic fit: little did I know that I would have to live for
such moments for the next fifteen years. For Dodger fans,
the pennant race was inevitably the spree and the World
Series (or playoff) was the hangover. But before I get into
some of the terrible things the Dodgers would proceed to
do to us refugees (no team has ever had more fans with
foreign accents), breaking our hearts in ways unknown to
Chinese torture and, incidentally, taking some of our minds
off the war for some of the time, I ought to mention that
there were some pretty good days too, and none better than

those last ones of September 1941, as we fended off the Cardinals and mopped up on the patsies in our own region, finally clinching against the Boston Bees and riding home to New York in triumph.

Again and again the story was told that year and the next of how Larry MacPhail, the choleric owner of the Dodgers, had taken his entourage to meet the train at 125th Street, but of how Durocher had unknowingly canceled the 125th Street stop—it was really a nothing station—in order to burst into Grand Central and get the orgy going as soon as possible. MacPhail had a red face even at the best of times —the kind of angry red that makes babies scream and sailors take warning—so it must have burst into flame as the train rattled past and disappeared in the direction of the party. "You're fired," he howled when he finally caught up with Durocher, deflating that indestructible man for the rest of the evening.

But there was no pain in it for the fans, it was all part of the Dodger harlequinade returning from a triumphant road trip with the clowns still flailing each other. MacPhail and Durocher were put on earth to entertain us, and if we had any doubts about that, they were erased forever the next morning when Larry called Leo, or so the story said, to discuss plans for next year, and Leo said he couldn't talk about them on account of he'd been fired, and MacPhail said, "Well, you're *un*fired." So the clowns embraced and Hilda Chester tolled her cowbell and the Dodger Sym-phony swung into "Happy Days Are Here Again." It all turned out to be part of a quaint courting ritual which would, after a whirlwind courtship, bind my ten-year-old soul to this organization with bonds stronger and more permanent than any enlightened religion insists on these days even for grown-up marriages. I was a Dodger fan forever. And I hadn't even met the girl yet, I'd only heard her described by Mr. Barber.

Little did I know that within a couple of weeks, the clowns would be tolling a funeral bell and the band would be playing "Goodnight, Ladies." The "better or worse" clause would be invoked early and often with the Dodgers. But that was okay the first time it happened, the bad news only strengthened the marriage, and the 1941 World Series debacle would actually help to convince me, like a harsh pinch on the arm, that I really *was* a Dodger fan and not just dreaming it. Anyone can root for a winner but it takes a stab of pain to initiate you all the way. As Mickey Owen dropped the third strike, and the guys in Father Anthony's room tried to explain to each other what was happening, a rite of passage occurred as surely as if blood had rolled down my finger. I was *in*. Which was not without its satisfaction.

Later as I compared notes with other fans, I learned that other teams did not necessarily insist on these barbaric rites as a prelude to becoming their fans. Yet even my favorite Yankee fan admits to a quickening during the 1944–45 years, when the Yankees became briefly as dreadful as anybody. Since rooting for that team was considered among decent people equivalent to rooting for General Motors or the British Empire—both of which could use rooters now —naturally these zombies treasured the pinch of pain that proved them human. It made them feel better about being sadistic front-runners for the next forty years. Or so we said. (People who have never lived in a three-team city will never know the giddy pleasure we used to get from slamming each other around with such insults, knowing we could hit as hard as we liked and never raise a real bruise.)

Yet finally, how blithely we all of us made these lifelong commitments. One guy would make his vows because a favorite teacher liked the Giants; another would bind himself over for life because there were more Italians on the Yankees right now. Becoming a Dodger fan in 1941 seems, in retrospect, like signing on for the Confederate army or the losing side in the Thirty Years War. You march into the recruiting office with a spring in your step and a song in your heart, expecting the glory to begin immediately. But then, there is a slight delay.

The delay that year, and then again and again, was caused by the abominable Yankees, a team which in retrospect gave us few rational grounds for hope that year, though what fan needs those, or even knows when he doesn't have them? Unlike some of the crazy-quilt lineups that Casey Stengel would stitch together after the war and somehow beat us with anyway, leaving us muttering in our beer like old Casey himself, this was a certified juggernaut that it was almost an honor to lose to. The Bronx Bombers (their name for the decade) had closed out the thirties with four world championships in a row, in a couple of which the other guy barely made it out of his corner but seemed to stand there waiting to be hit like King Levinsky against Joe Louis. Then after taking a year off in 1940, presumably just too bored to go on, they had burst back fresh as a daisy, or a shark that's missed a meal, in time for us.

Comparing the Yankee teams between the wars is a bit like judging a beauty contest that includes Hedy Lamarr, Marilyn Monroe, and Michelle Pfeiffer: it depends what you're in the mood for that day. The famous 1927 lineup was, of course, almost perfect but it could have used a better shortstop and catcher than Mark Koenig and Benny Bengough; but then by the time Frank Crosetti and Bill Dickey arrived to fill those holes, the dream outfield was no more. And by the time Red Ruffing and Lefty Gomez had hit their stride, Babe Ruth himself was gone.

And so it proceeded like a game played by history in order to keep you in the bar another hour or so in order to settle this thing once and for all. Someone was always entering the front door as someone else was being carried out the back. Tony Lazzeri loses it, Joe Gordon picks it up; Tommy Henrich walks in, but oh my God there's something the matter with Lou Gehrig; Charley Keller rushes to the scene, but . . . in short, like the city they played in, the teams would have been utterly perfect if they'd ever got it finished.

As it was, the 1941 edition had to settle for an All-Star or near-miss at every position except first, which area would remain more or less vacant for several more years in honor of Gehrig—whoever played there, be he Babe Dahlgren or that year's palooka Johnny Sturm or the next year's Buddy Hasset, began to shrink respectfully the moment he stepped on that hallowed ground; and weakness number 2, they had to make do with a second-drawer left-handed starter in Marius Russo in place of the fading Lefty Gomez. Big deal. They had Tiny Bonham and Spud Chandler to pitch for them now, and in the strange way of World Series, Marius Russo would inflict more damage on us than any of the big names anyway.

The Yankees of 1941 had already, before the Series began and from just watching out the corner of my eye, taught me a brand-new emotion, which, like the brutal horse-play of fans, seems to work better in sports than in life: total respect for one's opponent. (Nowadays when I feel this emotion, I'm tempted to change sides immediately.)

So—if they were that good, why did they have to stoop to being lucky in order to win?

Father Anthony's room filled up at last for the World Series, and guys who had expressed nothing but disdain for base-

ball suddenly revealed themselves to have been Yankee fans
and Dodger fans all along. And for the first four days of the
five-day Series, they rooted as convincingly as their total
ignorance of the two teams and their tendency to drift in
and out of the room piping "What's happening, did anything happen yet?" permitted. Then something awful happened in the fourth game and the flickering bulb of their
attention went out: their interest in major-league baseball
was dead for the year.

"Hey, there's still another game, maybe three. The
Dodgers still have a chance," I said after that fourth game.

"Yeah, sure." The corpse refused to stir.

And it wasn't just my schoolmates. The newspapers which
I had assumed would devote at least a week to dissecting
this tragic event gave it just one day before abandoning
baseball completely as if it had never happened, or worse,
as if it didn't really matter, once again leaving me to my own
dark thoughts.

Which weren't altogether dark after I'd worked them
round to the light for a while. Look at it this way. It was the
first Dodger pennant in twenty-one years—so what did I
expect, egg in my beer? Second, we had those guys on the
ropes not once but twice. After splitting the first two games
in the Stadium, a triumph in itself, we had them shut out
after six innings of the third game with "Fat Freddy" Fitzsimmons cruising on the mound, courtesy of what was still
virtually a secret weapon, the knuckleball. No *way* they
were going to get to Freddy.

So the lower-case bums resorted to luck. The one type of
hitter the knuckler is not proof against is a lousy one, so it
fell to Marius Russo the pitcher to disarm our hero with a
sneaky, contemptible line drive off his kneecap, the only
part of Freddy that wasn't cushioned, an Achilles heel in the
wrong place at the wrong time. As the radio voice described

this calamity, I recall it accelerating in excited horror, the way it might for an assassination attempt, and in my dreams I can hear myself shout "Jump, Fred! Why didn't you jump?" But nobody ever said anything about jumping when Freddy took this job and it was too late to bring it up now. So the Yankees scored two tainted runs and we scored one honorable one, and that was that. 2–1. All runs look alike in the record book.

But if Fitzsimmons (who'd been a great pitcher for the Giants, and for us too) couldn't jump, Mickey Owen *could* hang on to pitches, anything that was thrown, in fact. A couple of years later, my father and I would chance to watch a Brooklyn game together and that good man, who didn't know enough to watch the game conventionally, would suddenly remark on how very efficient the Dodger catcher seemed. Since nothing had happened that would appear to the untrained eye to distinguish one catcher from another —no dives into the dirt or into the stands, no runners caught stealing—this obviously meant that the Dodger man simply did the routine stuff perfectly.

Well, would that he did. For a split of a split second that super-efficient catcher held my whole happiness for the coming winter in the palm of his mitt—or so I pictured it: remember, all this is just words coming out of a box, I've never *seen* any of it—only to let it spin away. "What happened, what happened?" The guys who hollered this and the guys who tried to answer them set up a clamor that kept any of us from figuring out what actually *had* happened for several crucial minutes. In that era of catchable pitches it was entirely possible to get as far with the game as I had without ever hearing of a batter running to first on a dropped third strike. What I did know was that the Yankees had somehow gotten lucky again, and that they wouldn't need a second chance. The rain of hits that followed Owen's failure to catch the third strike and Henrich's gleeful scamper to first base were so much to be expected that I barely took in who did what after that—Keller, DiMaggio, Gordon, who cared. Mickey Owen had done it, and I would cry all winter.

That Mickey Owen, too, might be due for a bad winter never occurred to me, but I'm afraid I would have thought it served him right. For all that year and many years to come, no one questioned the man's total guilt: he had choked unforgivably, and would have to live out the rest of his life in the shadows, hoping that strangers wouldn't recognize him.

It was only long after the bodies were cold and the lynch mobs had dispersed that the revisionist historians set to work rehabilitating old Mickey. The most popular theory was that Hugh Casey, a troubled character who once had a crazy fight with Ernest Hemingway and later shot himself in the head like Papa, must have thrown a spitball—otherwise what in blazes was "Old Reliable" Tommy Henrich doing swinging at such a peculiar pitch? At the very least, Casey must have crossed up Owen's signs, throwing a curve instead of a fastball—and I'm not sure how it all wound up, except I know that Owen himself, who had prospered mightily in the intervening years and had become a Republican sheriff in Missouri, said at some point that it was just a good pitch that got away. Being a good sport had been kind to Mickey and he wasn't about to change now.

All this calming and cooling palaver was no help to me back then in October 1941 as I strove frantically, a hot-stove league of one, to do my own revisionism on the late World Series. Like an Arab dictator, I could always comfort myself that my people had stood toe-to-toe with the great Satan and given him what we took to be a scare. Our one mistake, as I said and kept saying, was letting the big guy off the ropes—but I'm not sure I quite believed it. Out of the corner of my eye, I could still see how quickly and surely the Old Nick pounced when the chance came, pounding the Dodgers into oblivion, and I guess even then I had to fight the fear that he would *always* find a way to come off the ropes. Right through the Series, I had felt as if we were trying to tame a man-eating tiger with a toy whip and a rubber chair as one legendary name came to bat after another. So we got Henrich, okay—who's next? Oh my God, it's DiMaggio—we got him too? Well, all *right!* Next victim. Charley *Keller?* You've got to be kidding. Just tell me—how many more times have we got to do this? *Eight?* I was almost tempted to drift out of the room myself. By some aural illusion, or sleight of ear, our guys seemed to shrink every time they failed to hit while their guys grew, as if each setback must be enraging them dangerously. So their eruption after Owen dropped the ball was precisely what my subconscious had been waiting for, and on that same level, I probably only wondered what had taken them so long.

There were good historical reasons for my defeatism. So far, I had rooted for nothing in life but underdogs, which was all very noble of me, but nothing whatever had led me to believe that they ever won anything. Although I knew for a fact that my guys had more laughs along the way and were much nicer people, I knew equally that there would always be Nazis, Bears, or (I apologize for my sense of proportion) Yankees waiting for them at the end of the story. Even the British successes in North Africa, and the apparent failure of the Blitz to defeat England on the spot, were only the equivalent of April victories in baseball (the war was not going to be settled in North Africa) and did not serve to offset the memory of jubilant Nazis goose-stepping through Paris in their own version of an end-zone strut. Life was like that, I very much feared.

. . .

Your nerves tell you one thing, your heart tells you another. Back in Torresdale a stray hound dog had followed me home one day that summer and sat on our porch until I came out so he could start following me again. Finally we decided to keep him, in the hunted sense that we couldn't get rid of him. And since he was strictly my dog and only followed me, and since he turned out to be a fiery little fellow who couldn't pass another dog of any size without trying to kill him, I named him Winston after Churchill and invested him with some of my own hopes and dreams. If I thought for one moment that the Germans were going to win this thing, I had only to take a walk with Winston and watch the other dogs, twice his size, shying away from him and cowering in their houses. A brave spirit and a homicidal glare could conquer anything.

The fact that in my absence that winter my parents had to have Winston put away by popular demand (and, I think, vague legal threats) was, I suppose, yet another lesson in who has the power around here: I trust at least that he bit the executioner and went down snarling. But the human mind is not symmetrical, and the experience of having owned such a dog at all was much more fortifying than his death was diminishing. My own little martyr would live on in my mind long after the fur had settled and the effete neighborhood dogs had come out of hiding and resumed their epicene ways.

All of which returns to me now as I try to reassemble the mood of willful pugnacity in the teeth of the evidence which disappointment in war, combined with the real Winston's speeches (and my own personal safety), had instilled in me by that indeterminate stage of world history. In such a mood, it was a cinch to twist a mere World Series into any shape I liked. The Dodgers had *much* better pitching than the Yanks, if only because they played in a pitchers' league; they had the best young player in baseball in Pete Reiser; they had in fact whatever I wanted them to have and they could keep it all winter. Above all the Bums were on the way up and the Bombers had to be on the way down soon —they had already defied gravity in staying on top as long as they had. Now they were down to winning on luck. The *Brooklyn Eagle* (soon alas to be extinct) had summed it all up very cleverly in a headline which was, believe it or not, once new: "Wait till next year." I couldn't have said it better myself.

With that taken care of, I regret to say, I forgot about baseball myself, unaware that already nesting enigmatically in the womb of winter was a new season that would convince me once and for all that underdogs do indeed win things—and that it could still hurt like hell.

However, football would not be denied any longer, but came bursting into my unformed psyche like some hearty jock in a turtleneck prancing around the room and insisting you come out and play with him. Well, okay! The air was crisp, the light was autumn-sharp, and running with your knees up against your chest suddenly seemed like the only possible thing to do.

In my tortured musings on the '41 World Series, as transcribed adultly, I seem to be crediting myself with preternatural powers of concentration and analysis in one so young, but this was not quite so. Reduced to a simpler notation, my thoughts could just as accurately have been rendered as a series of inchoate grunts and moans dressed up to go in words like "ouch" and "gotcha" and "What's next?"—words that could be transferred even more tellingly to football. So let's go, girls, our team's better than your team and hold that line. (Sis-boom-bah!)

The emergence of anything like full rationality is hard to chart retrospectively: at one moment, it seems to be a dim light bobbing in the fog; at another it's right in the room with you. It's there, you've arrived. And next day it's gone again. When I saw *The Maltese Falcon* around then, I knew right away that it was good in exactly the same way that I know it now—and I also knew that Bogart's next film was a disappointment. Yet when I saw the Three Stooges, I dissolved into a puddle of amorphous, pre-infantile glee—and it's *not* true that I still do. (Don't try me on Laurel and Hardy, though.)

And so it went with sports. So far as I can judge, I was already a far more mature baseball fan than a football one, and would remain so until I saw the Chicago Bears in person in 1942 and underwent a Newtonian revelation.

But there was no way you were going to experience such a revelation from the team I saw most of that fall. Since my weekends home from school ran from Friday night to Sunday lunch, I was unable to see any pro football and had to make do with the University of Pennsylvania Quakers, who were not at all bad in those days, but not at all interesting either. For years their coach, George Munger, doggedly hung on to the single-wing formation, as if his inner light instructed him to, until it would at last attain a certain antique value. But in 1941, everyone was still doing it, and no one did it more *averagely* than our Quakers.

To be fair, to be exciting in *anyone's* hands, the single-wing requires a tailback who lights up the sky, and Frank Reagan had graduated last year. Later, runners like Bobby O'Dell and Joe Kane would show some nice moves, but in '41 I don't remember any moves at all, except for some heart-stopping cumbersome double and triple reverses that, I'll swear, always lost at least 5 yards after 45 yards of lateral motion. Time seemed to stand still as Penn unveiled these prehistoric specimens of razzle-dazzle: the French artillery moved faster in plugging the holes gouged by the German tanks in 1940.

But the cerebellum can always dumb down if need be to accept new experience, and needless to say I was all agog over triple reverses, imagining them to be the height of human ingenuity, and I would be thrilled all over again when we tried to execute them, even more cumbersomely, at school.

Also nesting in the capacious womb of that improbable winter, along with World War II (American edition), was the whole modern game of football, with its arsenal of marvels all shiny and ready for use. Already there were hints of it in the college football magazines I had picked up that fall. Clark Shaughnessy, the closest thing to a father the T-formation had, had already installed his baby at Stanford, making instant stars of his quarterback, Frankie Albert, and his ace running back, Clark Gelineau; and then Frank Leahy had followed suit at Boston College, similarly transubstantiating Charlie O'Rourke and Mike Holovak. These and a handful of other T-formation pioneers have it in common with each other that they can never be satisfactorily compared with the stars of other eras because in their best years they weren't playing quite the same game as their contemporaries, but were a good two evolutionary steps ahead of them.

Meanwhile my school moved swiftly to install the Notre Dame shift, a formation that had galvanized the nation when Knute Rockne was young and mankind was cautiously climbing down from the trees. (I suppose the monks must have thought that it was a fine Catholic formation.) As far as my schoolmates were concerned there was only one college anyway and really only one game, to wit, the Notre Dame–Army game, which was played every year at Yankee Stadium in those days, briefly turning every New Yorker who knew what was good for him into a "subway alumnus" of the Irish, as the Slavs and Serbo-Croatians of Notre Dame were quaintly called. Needless to say my schoolmates, those baseball fans for a day, had no trouble with this, but became quite rabid rooters for so long as their attention spans permitted, while enjoying a snigger over the various parodies. "Tears, tears for old Notre Dame, the Poles and the Ginnies are stealing your fame," yok, yok, yok (no one ever seemed to mind having his own ethnic name thrown into the hopper, though I could have lived without "Limey").

I guess something about this compulsory adulation put my back up—people were supposed to disagree about sports, not fall in line like this: there was something bullying, maybe even threatening, about a roomful of guys who assume you agree with them about something as arbitrary as a game.

Yet how unthreatening it turned out to be when I finally got up the nerve to stick my neck out and do my underdog thing. "Hey guys, Sheed is rooting for Army." "You're kidding—*Army?*" "Yeah? Well what do Limeys know anyway?" "They probably wished they had an army themselves." The piling on at that age was as light as feathers, or the leaves that fell on Alice as she woke up from Wonderland. If your team lost, every disaster would be spun in your direction, as if the game were being played against you personally: but this in a perverse kind of way made you okay. "I thought Americans liked individualists." "Yeah, but not crazy ones." Losing was on the whole better, or at least safer, than winning, which made you a wise guy.

But the reel is spinning ahead of itself here, and flying through the years and through various rooms and bars, where the kidding becomes harsher and being a wise guy can get you into more trouble than it's worth. Demon rum, or demon money, or simply the squalls of adolescence can occasionally turn this kind of play-by-play drollery into the most dangerous sport since cock-fighting, breaking up friendships and jawbones and leaving a terrible mess to clean up later. But we're looking here at embryos, un-formed fans or non-fans, with the rationality variously fad-ing in and fading out, as they schlump through an afternoon the best they know how, innocently mouthing lines that could get them killed in later years.

That is to say, everyone who cares is mouthing them. As for the rest—when Jean-Paul Sartre said that "Hell is other people," he must have been talking about the people at sports events. Nowadays when I watch the Super Bowl, the host-person sternly maintains one serious room and one silly room, but try imposing a distinction like that when you're ten. "Hey Gilhooley, cut that out!"—a spitball has just creased the back of your neck but you try to stay calm, the way you do around stinging insects. "Hey Murphy—can't you guys do that stuff outside? It looks great out there." "We *like* it here. Who's winning, somebody? Hey, and who's *playing*, somebody?" Every room is a silly room when you're ten.

Every true sports fan is a solitary. "I did not love as others do," my father used to recite mockingly—"none ever did, that I heard tell on." And that's how it goes with sports. Sports haters are all alike but all true believers are happy in their own crotchety way, and I could only pray that these clowns would vanish soon or be struck dumb or grow up or all three.

I don't know quite how I got there, but by early Decem-ber I had my wish and was back by myself listening to the radio in the downstairs study in Torresdale, when I heard the only interesting thing to come out of a football game all season. The Eagles were playing the Redskins, so it sure as hell wasn't the game itself (although the Eagles kept the score miraculously close: down 14–7 was a Roman triumph for us against *any* opponent). But at halftime, the announcer, as if frantic to whip up any conceivable bit of excitement he could, announced that "this morning Pearl Harbor was bombed," a message that my friends tell me was also delivered at the Giants–Bears game that afternoon. The fact that none of us suspected that Orson Welles had a hand in the announcement may indicate how prepared we deep-down were for it: the only element of pure off-the-wall fantasy about it was the extent of the damage.

I wish that I could say that I grew serious on the spot and lost all interest in football for at least the rest of the day. But I have a sneaky telltale trace of a memory that tells me it wasn't quite so—that after the preliminary whoops of pleasure because America was now at war too, and after my less sincere expressions of regret that the creeps had to go and sink all those great ships for it to happen (you get used to living with radio and newspaper death a lot faster than TV death and it never occurred to me that this was a *human* tragedy), I fell to worrying about the dreadful possibility that the second half of the game might be canceled. It is, I guess, a sign of maturity, of which I've experienced surprisingly few in life, that I did not feel thus torn when President Kennedy was killed but spluttered indignantly along with everybody else when the National Football League decided to play its games as usual that Sunday "because he would have wanted it." (If anyone's listening, I don't want any games played when I die for at least ten years.)

Once the game was safely over, I rejoined the rest of the human race and my family, which was right then speculating anxiously as to whether "a state of war with Japan" automatically included Germany. Just fighting Japan got us nowhere, of course. A lot of good ballplayers would be drafted, and England would still be up the same old creek.

President Roosevelt's lordly declaration of war the next day put absolutely everything to rest—except for the ballplayers being drafted, of course—and in the majesty of the moment, I felt I could face that sacrifice too. What the heck, it was mid-winter, and baseball was still light-years and several millennia away. With the United States in the war, it would surely be over by spring.

So now, let's get serious and win this thing. Like all good ten-year-olds I was nuts about Roosevelt. I had campaigned for him in the last election to anyone who'd listen because his voice suggested that *everything was going to be all right,* whatever it was. Where Churchill made you want to go out and punch someone, Roosevelt made you sit back and purr. And where Churchill called for blood and tears, Roosevelt told you it was in the bag. No contest. Capable hands—the phrase was made for FDR. We were in capable hands now.

Two years later, our school staged a debate and I found myself, incredibly, face-to-face with a couple of boys who claimed not to like Roosevelt. They said, of all things, that he paid farmers to burn their own crops, which struck me as not only a dastardly and improbable accusation, but basically beside the point. What about the war? Well, there was that, they conceded—it was still too soon for such boys to say "He lied us into war," though they would be ready for it—but they conveyed the strange impression that the war wasn't that big a deal. We had problems over here too, and we couldn't go on solving them with a policy of "spend, spend, spend—elect, elect, elect." What I remember best now is their placid good humor in the face of my trumped-up pseudo-Churchillian passion, which they countered with portentous bits of paper that one of them drew in the manner of Spencer Tracy from, no doubt, his father's briefcase. "Report from the U.S. Department of Agriculture, March, 1937, p. 198 passim." I had hit the rock of American isolationism and for several days my hands wrung from the encounter.

Yet perhaps that easygoing self-absorption suited me better than I cared to admit. What could you do with such people? Just as the good life now consists of being the only reform Democrat in a town full of Republicans, so it was no bad thing back then to be the school's most serious warrior. Two years or so before this debate, in the stark summer of 1940, I would not have let my opponents, or myself, off so lightly, but would have screamed in rage and disbelief at the incurable triviality of Americans—but that was before Mr. Roosevelt took us in his hands, and began to tap into America's vast reserves of optimism and goofy overconfidence, of which there was easily enough to fill the tank of a pint-sized refugee: a man who could chat us out of a major depression could surely sweet-talk us double-quick through a major war. In fact, I can almost imagine my 1942-self telling my 1940-version to "lighten up," if we had used the phrase back then.

In this vein, I also thought that FDR's most statesmanlike decision of that period was giving baseball the green light. Now that was very wise—obviously we needed our morale turned up high as we saved our tinfoil and used fats (whatever they were) and buttoned our lips lest we sink ships. (I didn't plan to tell anybody *anything*.) And what were 400 ballplayers out of a populace of 120 million anyway?

Later, of course, Roosevelt would betray me too, by allowing "the 400" to be drafted willy-nilly like everybody else, leaving baseball looking like one of the cars people drove in wartime, all patched up and wheezing. What good was a green light if you couldn't get the car to start? And how was a guy to keep up his tinfoil collection on a diet of Joe Buzas and Eddie Bazinski? It would be small comfort to learn that, by typical sleight of hand, FDR—who signed his cables to Churchill "Naval Person"—had simply slid all the best players over to the Great Lakes Naval Base, where they would form the greatest baseball team in the whole of human history, and give us no doubt the world's most cheerful navy (and don't tell me Roosevelt, the old secretary of the navy, didn't know about it).

Anyway, a fat lot of good such shenanigans did me and my friends who were forced to grow up during the greatest drought in baseball history. You can still wring a bitter laugh out of any right-thinking member of my generation by saying the magic names "Ossie Grimes . . . Phil Weintraub . . . Howie Shultz." Some of these, like Weintraub, were actually pretty good ballplayers, who'd been coaxed off their rockers for a last spin around the Bigs: but the great washing machine of history has long since flung them together into a soggy clump called "wartime baseball"—a phrase which can wring a laugh all by itself.

If I had foreseen all that on the morning of December 8th, it would surely have clouded my day. But at that point, and with President Feelgood manning the fireside, a four-season war was simply out of the question. Roosevelt could make you feel better about going to war than you had ever felt in peacetime, and I remember that winter with peculiar pleasure, as we plunged about in the wet snow, sliding into snowbanks and washing away our tiny troubles. There is nothing like snow for simplifying life; it is the symbol of amnesia and stupidity. "My mind went blank." And when it filled again, it was with the sight of guys throwing baseballs between the drifts and the sweet sound of ash on horsehide. This was going to be a *great* year!

And it was, too. Up to a point.

4

The Year of the Cardinals

Roosevelt seemed at first to mean what he said about a green light, and 1942 turned out to be almost indistinguishable from a regular season, and a superb one at that. Like a plague that was just clearing its throat, the war swooped and seized a player here and another there, taking Henrich off the Yankees, which was only fair, and Sam Chapman off the A's, which wasn't, and then quite viciously stripping the Washington Senators, of all people, of Cecil Travis and Buddy Lewis, their only two stars—but in general causing no more damage than injuries might in a normal year. The draft simply turned the screws on the tension of the National League pennant races (might we conceivably lose

Pete Reiser?), making it altogether the tensest, and most intense, experience of my whole sports life.

There would be reasons for this beyond the generous merits of the 1942 season. "It's all right to read them once, but that's quite enough." A year or so later, my father would come across my cache of *Baseball* magazines, and perhaps gauge from the density of the thumbprints that all my modest reading time had been turned over to them. This, he made clear, would have to stop: from now on I must at least *pretend* to have other interests—and perhaps from pretending hard enough, actually acquire some.

But in 1942, "they" left me alone. My father had just beaten back the comic-book menace, which was all right with me (I could always catch up with them at school), and he was always on guard against playing the tyrant. American children led intolerably sloppy and dissipated lives by English standards, with their weekly movies and their nightly radio and their simple-minded picture-books, but he couldn't stanch the whole tide single-handed. He must have sensed early on that if he came on like even the most liberal of English fathers, it would play like Caligula over here.

And besides, he had a weakness for sports himself, if not American ones, and if not all the way around the clock and calendar.

So for that one year, baseball had me to itself, all the more intensely because it was still mostly in the head. The monks at school had decreed that our little hands were too small and fragile for hardball, so we'd been obliged instead to try wrapping them around softballs, which were about right in size for my two-handed set-shot and gave no hint of the gut joy of playing baseball, which depended on *precisely* that size of ball, as it depends on just those relative distances between the bases. (Relative, because although 90 feet is fixed in the stars for grown-ups, new lengths must be determined for kids, but on the same principle: the distances must leave just enough time for double plays.)

Then back in Torresdale, my guru Johnny Horan, who had taught me the ABCs, that is, to hold my bat *off* the shoulder and to stride straight into the pitch and not in the vague direction of left field (easier said than done), was only available on rare occasions. And there wasn't too much else. So it was back to Mike Kreevich and tinkering with my batting stance and praying that some one of my aged neighbors would miraculously rear back and give birth, like Sarah in the Bible, to a boy who would even more miraculously emerge at about my own age and not turn out to be a butterfly collector or other form of creep. I would also have welcomed, with happy tears and glad cries, the most sadistic Little League coach ever devised if he could have led me out of this wilderness and into one genuinely honest-to-God (and is it too much to ask?) baseball game.

Forget it. Wartime made the village even older, as our few borderline middle-aged members thought of something that needed doing in the army or in Washington. The advent of gas and tire rationing meant that the only people to remain in communities like ours were people who preferred to stay put anyway and fan themselves on the verandah, while I pounded feverishly up and down our lawn wielding alternately a lawn mower and a baseball bat. "Now I'm Dick Siebert . . . how's this for a Foxx?" When you're not facing pitching, one stance is precisely as good as another, since you have all the time in the world to straighten up and swing like a normal person. But with none of my stances could I master the knack known to every potbellied coach in baseball of stroking the ball to within a few feet of where I wanted. Instead my whooshing, wheeling swings came reasonably close to simulating game conditions, as a motley assortment of liners and grounders and pop-ups came streaming off my heaving, overweight bat. I may even be the only fungo hitter in history to accomplish the feat of striking himself out, as frustration gave way to blinding rage and I swung at my own increasingly bad pitches.

As I imagine myself now watching in long-shot from our kitchen window in Torresdale, I can say with some certainty that the kid is neither unhappy nor altogether wasting his time. As the extrovert languishes, the introvert comes into his kingdom, and the first stories I told myself were baseball stories—no, I should make that second, because in England, I had already been a member of Robin Hood's gang in Sherwood Forest, a cross between Little John and Robin Adair the troubadour, which may sound like richer subject matter than baseball, but wasn't really. All I could think of to do in Sherwood Forest was run through the trees and shoot my arrows and jump on the sheriff's back. Good stories are hard to come by in any setting, as I was reminded when I finally saw an Indiana Jones movie and observed that it consisted of nothing but narrow escapes, a story form as cramped as any locker room.

So be it. Since my imagination never did have the budget of a Steven Spielberg, I was more than content with my new minimalist world of imaginary pennant races and ninth-inning rallies. My version of Indiana Jones had narrow escapes too, variously pitching out of jams and getting caught in rundowns and pivoting into the flashing spikes of his mortal enemy. He was sometimes a kid trying to make good and sometimes an old man trying to hang on; he was everything I knew. The child storyteller has so little of real life to work with anyway that he might as well use baseball, he won't exhaust it in a hurry, and it wasn't until I was fifteen that I began to worry about the narrowness of my fixation and the bareness of the tales I told myself every night to put me to sleep. But by then, it was either that or sex, and my religion did not forbid me to think about baseball. So I squeezed another year or so out of baseball before discarding it—for cricket. But we'll get to that in a minute.

Nineteen forty-two was also a year when the war in Europe held its breath. (Russia didn't count. What happened in Russia was that the Germans would keep going until they got stuck in the snow. Everybody knew that.) Otherwise—England seemed to be out of danger, the Second Front was at least a year away, and America was still working on its morale. And I hadn't learned yet to consider the Pacific part of the same war. Even so pure an obsession as my baseball one prefers a vacuum, and there never was such a vacuum as my edited version of 1942.

So what have we here? The A's were going to miss Sam Chapman badly, the draft people obviously didn't give a damn about competitive balance in the American League, but war is hell, I know, I know: so who else had lost what? The first blissful weeks of baseball awareness as the game shakes off sleep and the teams assemble in Florida for roll call and the sports pages begin to phase out indoor track meets and fill up with a *real* sport were largely spent counting arms and legs that year.

The Dodgers, stop right there, seemed to be more or less intact. Cookie Lavagetto had gone into the navy, little knowing that he had an appointment with history soon after he got out. Too bad—the knowledge would have given him a wonderful war. And we seemed to be missing Luke "Hot Potato" Hamlin, a swell middle-relief man and spare-parts starter. But war is etc., and to offset these lessons, we had acquired Floyd "Arky" Vaughan, soon to be my all-time hero, over the winter, and the Cardinals had voluntarily given up Johnny "Big Cat" Mize, trading him to the Giants in what had to be his prime.

What was wrong with him? the papers wondered, and

what was Mr. Rickey's game this time? The sainted Branch, whose sanctity up to that point seemed to consist entirely of not watching baseball on Sundays, although he accepted the receipts, had a reputation for trading slightly damaged goods guaranteed to fall apart on arrival—his *pièce de résistance* being Dizzy Dean's sore arm, shipped to the Cubs virtually in splints and ice for four healthy players and cash. So it was generally assumed that Mize had gone quietly blind during the winter, or lost a leg in a hunting accident. Anyway, he was out of there, and the track seemed clear for the Dodger cannonball. Indeed, it was probably none too soon to start scouting the Yankees for the Series—although what was to scout? The same old perfection.

I was right about the Yankees anyway. Although it was, as I would learn more often than I strictly needed, just possible to be overconfident about the Dodgers, you could not be overconfident about the Yankees: a Yankee fan could order his World Series tickets in April, and devote the balance of the season to looking for extraterrestrials with gambling problems to bet with.

So heigh-ho for another subway series, and how about the Athletics for a strong second in the American League. Third maybe? Fourth would be okay—there is no point in dragging this out and suffering all over again. Thinking about it brings me out in acne and colic and other infantile disorders. It seems the damn team had peaked *last* year, when it won 64 games and finished a scant 37 games out of first place. In '42 the numbers would be 55 won and 48 out and sinking. What I had taken in the spring to be signs of life were really death rattles.

If you can stand a moment of Athletic trivia: Mr. Mack had stirred in his sleep long enough to trade the still flourishing Wally Moses to the White Sox for two nonentities from the rich Chicago School and cash. But the trades he didn't make were probably worse. Dick Siebert dropped from .334 to .260 that year (even such careers as his have "career years"), Bob Johnson hit .291 but had apparently lost his home run range-finder for good, and Frankie Hayes slipped enough to be traded to the Browns halfway through the season when his decline was already out there for all to see. If Rickey shipped his stars out a year too soon, Mack at that stage had to hustle to be only a year too late.

Those who have never tried it will never know the vast difference between finishing a promising last and a hopeless one. After the season, fate would give us a last playful kick in the head the way Elisha Cook used to do in the movies when he had Sam Spade on the floor, by tapping our ace pitcher Phil Marchildon on the shoulder and whisking him off to join of all things the Canadian air force, an outfit that will obviously do anything for attention (I see no reason to be fair about this). Like other last-place fans, we already were down to eating crumbs off the rug, and the loss of Marchildon didn't leave much: Elmer Valo in right looked okay. A couple of the infielders, Pete Suder and Buddy Blair, would not have looked out of place on a *sixth*-place team. And for pitchers—well, Roger Wolff and Russ Christopher did manage to give Ted Williams a hard time with the knuckleball one afternoon, striking him out or popping up consistently until the tenth inning of the second game, when he solved this exotic pitch once and for all with a lordly poke over the right-field wall. And that was about it for the A's in wartime.

In Philadelphia we didn't bother to say "Wait till next year," because next year was usually too horrible to contemplate; instead we said, "Remember Howard Ehmke, huh? Remember the ten-run rally?" So deeply screwed up and inverted was our relationship to the national sport and hence to life itself that we were probably the only part of the country that viewed the autumn of 1929 with pleasure. The onset of the Depression was the good old days, the rest was gall and wormwood. Like Rose of Washington Square, we had "no future but oh, what a past," and when our team was finally shipped off more dead than alive to Kansas City a few years later, it still seemed to be facing resolutely backwards.

Thank God I had balanced my portfolio with the Brooklyn Dodgers. Rooting for two teams introduces you to the subtle condition of the mixed day, in which it's entirely possible to feel both elated and shattered at the self-same moment, as one of your horses comes from behind to win at Belmont even as the other blows an unbeatable lead at Monmouth Park. Although your common or garden two-team parley never induced the schizophrenia routine to today's rotisserie leagues, which pit pitchers owned by you against hitters owned by you in an equation that no one else in the stands is even aware of ("What the hell *you* cheering about, mister?"), it was almost enough to splinter the skull of an eleven-year-old. If the test of a first-rate mind is its ability to entertain two different ideas at the same time, by the end of the year I was Einstein. Because by that time, I was juggling three.

How we arrived at that ending, I'll never quite understand. As early as June, the season looked like an open-and-shut case. In a word, the Brooklyns were breezing, and in the process slowly weaning me away from the American League for good—although I continued to root for it in the All-Star Game a couple of years longer (and how's that for first-rate thinking?). Since my mixed days consisted mostly of Dodger wins and Athletic losses, and since I wanted to make these days as painless as possible, it only made sense to lean my weight more and more on the Dodger side of the scale until, with the transfer complete, the whole thing tipped over inexplicably in August and went crashing to the ground, leaving me more desolate than just rooting for the sad sack A's could ever have done. In baseball at least, it is infinitely better never to have won at all than to have won and then lost—as evidenced by the goofy good nature of Cub fans through the miserable years and the querulous crabbiness of Met fans after they won it all in 1986 and came up empty the next few summers. (To make the contrast even sharper, you need only compare Mets fans with each other between 1985 and 1987: no chemistry set ever turned men into beasts faster.)

None of this morbid, Ingmar Bergman on a rainy day type of wisdom was anywhere in sight, though, when the Dodgers came to town to play the Phillies in a July 4th double-header and I got to see my love objects in the flesh for the first time. It was like an arranged marriage, in which you don't get to meet the other party until it's too late—was it conceivable that I wouldn't like these guys? Well, hardly, since I'd arranged the match myself. Still it was a relief to find them even more charming than I expected.

July 4th is a perfect day for a ball game anyway, and an even better one for two (my blood runs cold, or refuses to run at all, at the thought of July 4th night games, an affliction introduced by the villainous Walter O'Malley, against whom this book is dedicated). The night before, the whole sky was ablaze with light, as the town joined in a fireworks salute to the visiting team. And then on the day itself, everybody who was anybody trooped over to the ballpark to celebrate the most totally holiday-holiday in the calendar.

This year would be the best of all. America's team would be playing America's game in the first year of America's war. Like all fresh wars only more so, this one had generated a reserve of extraneous excitement, like the excess heat off an engine, so that everything you did this year was a little more exciting than usual. Seeing Ingrid Bergman in *Casablanca,* for instance. (A curious experience. Something had changed. The stakes were raised.) There was a hubbubbleburble in the stands that day of a kind not usually associated with the Phillies, mainly because the stands were usually empty for their games: but this was war! And the light that Gatsby saw at the end of the dock was obviously the green light Roosevelt was waving at baseball.

Gatsby was even right about the orgiastic future. The Dodgers won the first game 14–0, and you can't get more orgiastic than that. For once, I don't remember the details, except for some elegant plays by Pee Wee Reese at short and a neat little home run by Pete Reiser which caused my father to exclaim "What superb timing," sweet praise indeed from a cricket lover. It was the first time we'd been to a game together, and I found my father's innocence of the game quite amusing. When, for instance, the Phils rallied in the second game to close the margin of defeat to a mere 5–4 behind the slugging of one Alban Glossop, he felt as *I* would have last year, that this team was on its way now and might henceforth be a contender to keep an eye on.

"Look," I explained patiently. "The Phillies will probably win maybe three games off the Dodgers this year. The Browns may even take two off the Yankees. It's no big deal in baseball. They are definitely not a team to keep an eye on." In those paper-rich days, the standings showed precisely how each team did against each other team, so I had already divined the relative closeness of the best to the worst in baseball. Except for the Yankees.

"As you say," my father said obligingly. It was his nature and his strategy to yield areas of expertise (a word he hated, incidentally, for its half-baked Frenchness) to his children, building us up that way without encouraging us to be know-it-alls. We knew one thing, he knew the rest. So he contented himself for now with the vexatious observation that he could never take altogether seriously a game that required grown men to wear those ridiculous trousers. So much for my area of expertise.

Trousers or no, the Dodgers looked just fine to me: Medwick with his foot raised and his bat seeming to project from his hip (an impossible style to imitate, or even describe); Vaughan, the new boy, with his feet splayed in the openest stance I've ever seen; Dixie Walker the classic, smooth left-hander; Billy Herman, Dolph Camilli—nobody was going to beat these guys this year or ever, and that went for the so-called New York Yankees *and* the Chicago Bears.

Apparently the Dodgers felt the same way themselves, because by early August, Larry MacPhail, who was a great baseball man, if a weird one, thought he had spotted a fatal smugness emanating from his team and hollered the boys into his office to tell them about it. "You boys think you're gonna win it in a walk? Well, you're not." And he offered, as was his wont, to bet any man in the house to that effect, and I guess I should have been bothered by the fact that only Walker took him up on it: I guess the others didn't want to take his money (when the story was published, I almost mailed my allowance to MacPhail and asked him to bet against that).

Now of course, this was no visit to *Steinbrenner's* office. MacPhail had hand-picked these guys himself from all around the league and he knew all there was to know about them. Nevertheless, the Dodgers *did* have an eight-game lead and it *was* mid-August, and MacPhail's wild-eyed prophecy would probably have gone the way of all boozy blather, or at best lived on as a footnote in some child psychology textbook, if it hadn't been for a miracle occurring many miles away, beyond the range of MacPhail's clairvoyance. As a matter of fact, the Dodgers *did* shape up after that, if they had ever needed to, and came pounding down the stretch with their tail in the air to win 104 games, enough to win a pennant in any season save two in history.

But a fat lot of good it did them, because this was one of the two. There are moments in history when human science can only throw up its hands and rend its smock and mutter "We just don't know." Old Cub and Orioles fans, for instance, may analyze till Hilda Chester's cow comes home just how in the world the New York Mets ever managed to beat their teams in 1969, but they're wasting their time. The Mets were beyond analysis that year: the god of one's choice sends us these things once or twice in a lifetime like a playful wind blowing our papers on the floor, to remind us who's in charge around here. The only thing is that if you were a Dodger fan, he kept on doing it year after year. (One of the joys of 1969 for transformed Dodger fans was the giddy experience of being on the winning end of one of these phenomena.)

What made the 1942 Cardinals a particularly galling team to lose to was that we were better than them on paper, and so far paper was all I knew. Box scores were fuller in those days, little masterpieces of storytelling in fact, but they did not record diving catches or kamikaze slides, and these were the very essence, the meat and potatoes and bread and butter of the '42 Cards—so much so that when they got through with you, they looked by their uniforms as if they'd been playing football and not baseball at all. In fact, Branch Rickey was so far beyond paper when he fashioned this team that he could have been thinking of Astroturf instead, which was only about twenty years off in the future, well within Rickey's range.

When I finally got to see the Cards that year it was with eyes blinded with loathing and dread, and I didn't take in from the two games I saw that Terry Moore in center and

Marty Marion at short had effectively cordoned off from traffic the two parts of the field to which the most balls are hit. Meanwhile, Enos Slaughter in right and Johnny Hopp at first had that lane pretty well blocked off as well, while Creepy Crespi and Jimmy Brown, who rotated at second, seemed like nothing more or less than the kind of guys you put in the game for purely defensive purposes. Billy Herman in his epic interview with Don Honig graphically described the frustration of flogging the ball into this safety net and realizing that nothing was going to get through today. Home plate was socked in.

I wish I'd known that at the time. Reading it some thirty years later I felt as one might on finally learning the *real* reason Hitler didn't invade England or the answer to some other problem that's been vaguely bothering you for years. So *that's* why everyone who pitched for the Cards seemed like Hall of Fame material. Mort Cooper of course, and Johnny Beazley obviously had to be great. Max Lanier too. But Howie Krist? Ernie White? Old Howie Gumbert?

All I knew was what I read in the paper, and without the game in front of you, all the credit goes to the pitcher, twirling his nifty eight-hitters or his gaudy six-hitters, as the pundits put it. So Howie Krist was a great pitcher, and that was that. Bear in mind, also, that I was just one child's year (which is equivalent to about seven adult years, or one dog year) away from believing that baseball was all hitting; since then, grudgingly, I had allowed pitching into the club. But there was no way I was going to accept fielding and base running as important. Get serious. Everyone in those days managed like Earl Weaver, and the team with the most home runs and 20-game winners won, it was a law of life.

There is no one more conventional than a small boy, so I was only echoing the received wisdom of my elders. And we were all, graybeards and tots alike, equally outraged to find that while we were talking, Mr. Rickey had stolen our pants. It had to be a trick, of course. Baseball could have learned a lot from Rickey's last Cardinal teams, but it was not up to moving its mental furniture so quickly—not so long as the Yankees were still around, advertising the virtues of the long ball and the quick fix. Instead, baseball, and me with it, rolled over in bed and went back to sleep for another decade or two.

Rickey-ball, with its emphasis on speed and defense and batteries of replaceable young pitchers, was like a T-formation that baseball was too stuck in its ways to accept yet. So I had no idea I was gazing into a Futurama exhibit worthy of the recent World's Fair when the Cards came to Philadelphia in early September, tied for first place with the Dodgers. What it *felt* like was a nightmare that won't quit: footsteps that keep getting closer and closer and you feel the fingers around your throat—but this time you *don't* wake up at the last second. The Cards had just won two in Brooklyn, searing the name Whitey Kurowski into my brain, and now they were here eyeball-to-eyeball with me, and choking me to death.

Kirby Higbe tells in his memoirs of how the day before the very double-header I saw, Durocher hired two of Philadelphia's finest hookers to go to work on one of the St. Louis pitchers who was due to start the next day and render him generally unfit for baseball. Leo was a great manager off the field too, with a head for details, and he probably instructed the ladies to jump up and down on the guy's pitching arm every chance they got. But it just wasn't Leo's year, because, as I saw with my own eyes, both Cardinal starters, whose names I have tactfully forgotten, ripped through the Phillies that afternoon while the Dodgers were

dropping two to Cincinnati. (On the other hand, the hookers reported in exhausted when Leo demanded his money
back.)

Misery on the field and misery on the scoreboard. There
was nothing mixed about that particular day. What I remember most clearly about it is the gathering certainty that
things weren't going to get any better. This nightmare had
to play itself out. All the callow fatalism I had picked up
from the fall of Paris on through Mickey Owen's passed ball
told me that stories like this did not turn happy at the end.
The only way to enjoy this kind of thing is to dive exuber-
antly into melancholy until you touch bottom, and just wal-
low. But I was new at it, and my misery had no company yet
(I didn't know a single other Dodger fan), and pound for
pound I was undoubtedly the unhappiest creature in the
history of the world that day.

Yet if you turned the kaleidoscope over on its head the
snow was actually falling in the right direction for once.
Whatever the Cardinals were—"upstarts," the word that
drove Groucho up the wall in *Duck Soup,* comes to mind
—they were not the favorites. For once in my life I had
made the mistake of betting against the underdog, and look
what it got me—a vicious beating behind the woodshed,
and scars that would last exactly three weeks. If, as my
(Irish-Australian) father used to say, "the Irish are no good
at being rich," then I was no good at being a front-runner
—the Yankees themselves would have sunk like a stone
with me on their backs—and I have pretty much avoided
the temptation ever since.

The rest of September was only a kind of logical conclu-
sion, or unraveling, of that day. The Dodgers quickly got
their feet untangled and began whomping people right and
left, but they wouldn't be going head-to-head with the Cards
again, and St. Louis proved just as deadly as they at beating

up on the league's underprivileged (no great accomplishment that year: the Braves and the Phils couldn't have climbed out of the second division if they'd stood on each other's shoulders). That Sunday had left the Cardinals two games, two strides, in front and that's the way they stayed, like Roger Bannister and John Landy lapping their way silently around the track in the Dream Mile at Vancouver in 1955, until they crossed the finish line one–two on the last day of the season—exactly two games apart.

The Dodgers in fact had had a hell of a September, but owing to their curious magnetic arrangement with the Cards, they had appeared to be standing still all along.

A year later, I would discover the poetry of John Keats—a monster distraction that would later lead me miles from baseball for days at a time—where I would find the first literary image ever to hit me right where I lived: that of a youth pursuing a maiden who is forever just out of reach. "Bold lover, never, never wilt thou kiss/though winning near the goal." Since both these characters appear to be painted on the side of a vase, the chances are considerably less than rosy that the guy will ever make time with this particular doll (I discovered Runyon that same year), but he is in the record book forever as a near-miss who gave it his best shot.

And that was my Dodgers, as they pursued their pennants and championships down the years—never, never (or hardly ever) to kiss them, however close they got. They didn't choke, they didn't fold. They just started waiting till next year a little too soon.

After you've been tortured long enough, the pain begins to let up or even to go into reverse, and as the days dwindled down, the sharp jabs to the kidneys that each Cardinal success delivered felt not much worse than the nails Hindu mystics sleep on in cartoons. The whole month seemed to be played in the shadow of that brooding Shibe Park score-board, which told me as sure as the Recording Angel that the Dodgers were not going to make it, and I might as well get on with my wallowing. The time was by no means wasted, for during the course of that quintessential mixed month, my masochism at least advanced by leaps and bounds until by the end of it I was almost a full-fledged Dodger fan. Which means that in a whining and breast-beating contest, only a Cub or a Red Sox fan could stay in the same ring, or living room, with me. The English won all the battles but the Irish went home with all the songs, and fans of these three (now alas two) mournful persuasions always seemed to get more fun out of the game than the world's winners will ever know.

But the train bursts out of the tunnel eventually and now it's October, a totally new season: not a dying summer any more, but a crisp spanking new autumn, with the other game already out of its cage and prancing across the sports pages, bursting its britches to take over. September in a last-place town is like the world's longest funeral ceremony. The crowds have long since gone home, leaving you alone by the graveside, and the shadows look longer than sky-scrapers and—is it your imagination, or are the players hurrying to get it over with? The veterans could be anyway, the rest you never heard of so who cares what they do? Unless one of the contenders is in town, the last-place team uses the shank of the season to dump the contents of its crumby farm system on the table, and the truth is, players you've never heard of never seem as good as famous ones, whatever they do that day.

Meanwhile, from all the way across town, your ears can just pick up the dying remains of a real crowd noise: Pennsylvania is playing Lafayette in its home opener. And maybe you should have used that ticket.

It is a season for betrayals and new beginnings. In towns like Wildwood, the boardwalk novelties are being dismantled or boarded up, and the girl you met there decides not to write after all, or if she does, the letter is cool as an autumn wind and full of new plans and names. But so are you, and she really wouldn't fit in.

This psychological background is the closest I can come to an excuse for my own modest stab at treason that October—treason of a kind that would get you shot if you did it to your country in wartime, but also of a kind that I have committed so many times since at the start of various Octobers that I'd like to name a feast day after it. In brief, I forgot all my grievances and rooted my brains out for the Cardinals.

Well, look at it this way, your honor. The Cardinals had beaten my real team, so if they lost now, what did that make the Dodgers—the *third* best team in baseball? Impossible. Second, the Cards *were* the underdogs, so I was in effect simply asking to be clobbered all over again, which is not a hanging offense in most states. And third, wasn't I supposed to love my enemies, huh?

These were perfectly good arguments—the first two anyway (I knew the third was a clinker the moment I thought it)—but they did not adequately explain my unholy enthusiasm for St. Louis as the Series progressed. From a standing start, I managed in no time to work up a head of enthusiasm that actually threatened to blow my head off in the sixth and seventh innings of game three (I can date the crisis precisely). By that time, I was deeply in love with this team and could barely recall ever loving anyone else. The very things

I had hated when they did them to the Dodgers—the base running, the defense—seemed quite charming when they did them to the Yanks. Welcome to National League baseball, sucker!

Every love affair introduces you to a new aspect of life, a new way of looking at things: before you met this girl you had never known a real Norwegian family, or talked to a practicing Buddhist, or tasted such meatballs or attended such weddings. In baseball terms, my Cardinal flings, of which I've since had several, were every bit as strange at first and disorienting as spending the evening with a girl of, let's say, mixed Latvian and Balinese origin.

St. Louis, bear in mind, was the closest thing to a Far West that big-league baseball permitted itself in those days: after that, you fell off the planet. St. Louis may seem just around the corner these days, but back then it was separated by a long, clanking train ride of a kind that takes you halfway across Russia or China, reminding you every inch of the way of the vast number of churches and cow pastures and scraggly baseball diamonds between here and there—a lot of room for things to happen and change, and a lot of time for you to change too. So you never got the feeling common to air travelers that you were arriving in the same town you just left. Every city was a separate civilization, walled off by sheer space—and none more so than St. Louis, the end of the line.

Of course, your English correspondent here still had to *imagine* these distances back then—by multiplying the distance between Torresdale and Philadelphia by infinity. But something about the way it's laid out town by town makes America seem like a big country even if you haven't seen that much of it. And I knew for sure that the Cardinals seemed different, at least as described in the press.

Although the Gashouse Gang had evaporated by now,

their spirit seemed to linger in the swagger and country boy cockiness of their descendants. It was reported that the latter-day Cards still played their own music in the clubhouse, using for the purpose the same old washboard that Pepper Martin had once made famous. So I guess you could call them the first country-and-western team, drawing their crazy energy from the Mississippi itself—the Jazz river, the music river. Above all, every generation of Redbirds from 1926 on down had given the impression that they collectively had never heard of their opponents back where they came from, and weren't about to be impressed. Just what we needed to take on these so-called New York Yankees.

And so it mostly came to pass in that little gem of a World Series. After stumbling out of the gate with four errors in the first game—as if they had heard of the Yanks after all— they returned to their ignorant, unimpressible ways, and scored four runs with two out in the ninth by way of atonement, which wasn't quite enough to win that one but served as a dandy warning shot.

Of the four-game sweep that followed, I recall mostly a sense of contentment maintained at a very high pitch. Sports events that last several days generate an impossible mixture of serenity and nervousness, of smugness over what you've just done and apprehension over what's coming next. What precisely is one to think upon tying for the lead with a 66 on the third day of the U.S. Open? Do you feel first good and then worried, or do you conceivably feel both at once? And if so, what do you call the resulting alloy?

Whatever it is, I remember it more vividly as I sit here savoring it all over again than I remember the Series itself, which like most of its kind quickly boiled itself down to a few high points—as if one's very subconscious practiced news selection. Again, I never saw any of the games (this time not even a newsreel afterwards) yet I could swear I remember Enos "Country" Slaughter hurtling against the right-field fence at Yankee Stadium—which I had also never seen—to spear Charley Keller's obvious home run in the seventh inning of the third game.

God really tipped his hand on that one. Terry Moore had already made one miracle catch robbing DiMag of a triple to end the sixth, and Musial needed another miracle to run down Gordon's ball in the seventh. So Slaughter's catch made it three in a row, a hat-trick of miracles with no normal plays in between. But what was God to do? Ernie White (7–5 on the season) was pitching for St. Lou and his teammates were only scoring two runs. So the Man upstairs had to pull out all the stops that day, and listening to it on the radio, I of course smelled blossoms when the trees were bare and felt the earth move and my heart stand still—unusual sensations so I'm told, but old hat for baseball fans.

After that little splurge, the Almighty clearly decided, in Yogi Berra's felicitous phrase, to "sit back and enjoy the ball game." The Cardinals had applied the nerve-deadening treatment described by Billy Herman, which leaves the patient feeling briefly that he's staring into an enormous baseball glove filled with glue, and although the Yankees did not go down quietly, they did go down all right, losing three in a row in their own stadium, the Palace itself, where usually no one challenged them and lived. To crown the indignity of it, the Cards ended the Series, to all intents and purposes—the last two outs were a formality—by impudently picking Joe Gordon off second, as they had ended the 1926 one throwing Babe Ruth out on an attempted steal.

Normal teams didn't even think of doing things like that to the Yankees, for fear of reprisals. But seeing as how it was the Cardinals, I'm only surprised that they didn't give Gordon a hotfoot and tie his shoelaces together as well. No respect at all. There must have been wild music on the washboard that night.

For myself, I celebrated quietly as befits a collaborationist, with an orange soda in the school tuck shop (we called it that), while all around me my schoolmates were already beating a hasty retreat into total forgetfulness, as if there were not a moment to lose. By March, they would be asking who won the Series last year, and by June they would have forgotten who even played in it, leaving such scraps of exotica to weirdos like me. So be it. As I edited events hastily, before forgetting them myself for a few months, I could see that the big thing was that the Dodgers had been vindicated by the Series and that I would have all winter to straighten out my own thinking, in the manner of a Communist truth squad working over a dissident, and resume hating the Cardinals as if nothing had happened.

But before I got very far with this, the Dodgers themselves decided to mess seriously with my head by out-betraying me and signing on Branch Rickey, the Great Satan himself, to bring his brand of baseball to Brooklyn. Years later I would understand these things better. Leo Durocher goes to the Giants, Sal Maglie comes to the Dodgers. Love thine enemy was the name of the game, and the crowds turned out to prove it. But back then it seemed like the Allies trading for Adolf Hitler, and I wanted no part of it, no matter *what* Adolf's average was.

Or did I? Turn the page for a stunning development.

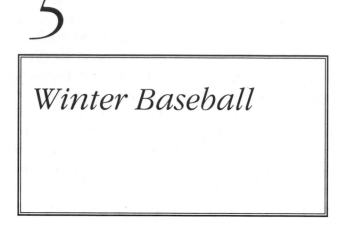

5

Winter Baseball

Well look at it this way.

Rickey's brand of baseball added to *our* brand of baseball would be pretty hard to beat, would it not? Darn right. Meanwhile, the Redskins were looking good this year and I had me a new hero, sight unseen—Sammy Baugh, the great Redskin tailback who, it turned out, was *every* kid's hero sight unseen.

Charles Dickens, whom I was just getting to know, had a maddening habit of opening every chapter with a change of subject: but so does sports, and the 1942 baseball chapter was closed. So next sport, please. I guess something about the name Sammy attached to the name Baugh, and something about his picture in the paper—we had to assemble our heroes out of primitive materials in the pre-TV era—plus the fact that he was the only potential giantkiller, or rather Bearkiller in sight, made Baugh briefly the Nation's Football Player, insofar as a professional could be. The NFL was still very much a poor relation of the colleges in 1942, but if you cared at all, you inevitably found yourself rooting for Baugh.

Not that it would do much good against the almighty Bears. Dr. Daley, my host to the football season, took me to see the Monsters of the Midway play the Eagles that year and you have never seen anything *quite* like it: a semi-evolved T-formation offense roaming at large, without a T-formation defense in sight to stop it. The only thing strange about the game was that for a while it seemed to be the Eagles, who had just installed the T themselves, who were doing the roaming. A 14–0 lead at halftime was absolutely as high as their inferiority complex would permit them to go, but it was dizzy stuff for us fans and although I was a hundred times more sophisticated and world-weary than I had been a year ago, I did think for a moment or two that, hey, maybe we were building a dynasty around here ourselves.

As a matter of fact, we were—but not that afternoon. The Bears came bursting from their dens in the second half, all the better for their nap, and before the shambles was over, they had buried our little dynasty 49–14, scoring apparently at will. It was, as advertised, a new kind of football, infinitely more exciting than the old—a fact that may not have escaped the dreamers of television who I imagine must have spent the war licking their chops and placing their bets on the boom that they knew was coming. The new formation would, it turned out, be so well suited to TV that it could have been designed in a studio.

But the T did still have a few glitches (which Paul Brown would take care of definitively at Cleveland), and there were days when you couldn't get the damn thing to start, and Baugh by God did kill the Bears later that fall to win the championship. I rounded out my little football season watching the Redskins take on the league's best players in what passed for an all-star game in that nine-team league. Sammy Baugh, in the manner of superstars, did not show up that day—another sixty minutes of two-way football on fragile legs was a lot to ask, and we forgave him—but it was a pretty good game anyway, with "Bullet" Bill Dudley running a kickoff back the length of the field and Merlyn Condit of the old Brooklyn Dodgers going about 70 yards with, what? a punt? an interception? I can see both men start their cuts, but they do it alone now on an almost empty field. The Redskins won 17–14 on the staccato line-bucks of Andy Farkas, and that was that, the short, sharp end of another chapter (the Bowl games that year are a total blank). After that, a few kids at school tried to talk about college basketball tournaments a little, but no one was listening: we had the bobsled out and the ice skates, and suddenly no one was a fan of anything any more but snow and more snow.

Except for your weirdo correspondent here. If this were a normal children's story, I would ask you to believe that at this point I heard a small voice coming from the baseball glove in the closet, saying "I'm still here." Because this was the year that baseball didn't leave after all; and whether the small voice was really as friendly as it sounded or was in fact pronouncing a serious curse on me I can never quite decide, because it hasn't left to this day.

In the hands of a Stephen King this could be a pretty horrible story—the baseball incubus that charms his way into your brain, and then insists on entertaining you until you scream for mercy. But in my version the host is a bit of a ghoul himself, the kind of guy who can't get enough of twenty-four-hour comedy cable channels or reading Dickens aloud in the jungle, so it's hard to say who is trapping whom—even when they take off for England together in 1946 and one of us has to teach the other cricket.

That winter, I turned twelve, which means I was just about fully developed as a fan. We mature early as a breed, somewhere between lyric poets, who I understood from my reading to be elderly gentlemen of eighteen or so, and chess players, who apparently hit their stride around four. Recently I chanced to reread an article on Ted Williams written by young Cleveland Amory in 1942, and was shocked to find myself reacting to it in exactly the same way as I had then, without any adult ironies or overtones or voices murmuring "Can't you see the writer is really saying this?" or "It's obvious that Williams was just a case of [name your favorite neurosis]": it was as if I had put the piece down the day before and face value was still quite good enough for me.

So what had gone wrong? Had I failed to grow up at all since then, or was I grown up already in that one respect? The answer in the case of Williams may simply be that in 1942 it was just a case of one twelve-year-old reading about another and life wasn't going to teach me a hell of a lot more about being twelve than I already knew. And this may be true of other superstars too whose inner resources have been entirely diverted into physical expression, like streams rushing into a great river. ("Did Fred Astaire ever say anything interesting?" says a friend. "Only every time he danced," say I.)

But there is a sense in which all we want from *any* of these guys is accessible to us at twelve. I'll take it on faith that some of them must have fascinating inner lives, but lots of people have those, and you don't have to dig so far to find them. What the jocks do have, and the first five reasons we're interested in them in the first place, is something quite unique to them—namely, the utmost physical skill under the utmost competitive pressure. And this is something you do appreciate at twelve with all the excitement and alertness of a fresh discovery. By that age, you have possibly had a chance to flinch at ground balls skidding at your face over pebbles or to stare down some testosterone freak from across a line of scrimmage, snorting sulfur and threatening to dismember you after the game. ("Under the stands . . . we'll be all alone." "Aah, your father's mustache.")

And then you go see Sammy Baugh passing the ball coolly through a wall of *enormous* testosterone freaks or, better yet, Joe DiMaggio tucking in his chin as a fastball whizzes under it, not deigning to fall down or so much as acknowledge the pitch one inch more than necessary. What more interesting thing are you ever going to learn about these men? When the great Bill Russell said, or snarled, "All I owe the public is a good performance," he was felt by certain heavy thinkers to be sloughing off his responsibilities, but in fact he was acknowledging them: Russell was one of those super-sensitives who threw up before all his games, which would take the fun out of most professions. So good performances didn't come lightly to him. And if you were a real fan, you were more than satisfied.

My sense of this may explain why my galloping obsession with baseball did not leave me with a great autograph collection, or any collection whatever. What you collected were moments framed in your head, pictures for the attic —the moments when these men are at their incandescent best, not when they're posing impatiently for photographers or scrawling their names absentmindedly. In the course of a lifetime, I would acquire precisely four baseball signatures on my own, and one through the mail, and lose them all. The first I got by tiptoeing timorously down to the roof of the A's dugout, expecting to be hurled back by an usher, to bum one off an expressionless Bob Johnson (actually, his eyes wandered, and I guess that's an expression); for the second and third I lined up in back of the Polo Grounds mostly because my friends were doing it, to get a Mel Ott and an Eddie Stanky (Ott was businesslike, Stanky surprisingly affable). And then to round out my lost set, I mooched out to right field in Bradenton, Florida, by now aged forty or so, to wheedle one off Roberto Clemente "for my son": he glared at me malevolently, as if to say "They all say that," and then to underline his contempt for grown men asking for autographs under any circumstances, started without preamble to do wind sprints to and from the place where I stood. Finding me still there, he reached for my pen—and all I had was a pencil.

Nothing could better have summed up my life as an autograph hound. Even as a kid, I only did it to meet the players, and now I didn't even want to do that especially, since I'd already met some athletes, and found their conversation almost as unrevealing as their signatures. However, before I could pay the Great Roberto back with a graceless snarl, he was accosted by three middle-aged ladies who'd come all the way from Allentown, Pennsylvania, to see him —and he was utterly charming and funny with them. So I learned something after all.

As for the autograph in the mail, it was actually a baseball signed by the whole Yankee team of 1943 from the office of general manager Ed Barrow, who shared a doctor with me. After the briefest of spiritual crises, in which I probed the

unthinkable—was it still possible to become a Yankee fan
after all I'd seen? I was still young, and in fact I'd only heard
about baseball four years ago: but no, it wasn't possible; my
bones were set and no bribe in the world can change a
baseball allegiance—I decided to use the damn thing for
the purpose which nature intended. What the hell, it was
wartime and baseballs were in short supply, especially big-
league ones. And it was a profound pleasure to lay the wood
on those arrogant names.

Which is not to say that my obsession used no props at all.
I sent away to *Baseball* magazine for pictures of my heroes
of the moment, Pete Reiser and Arky Vaughan—but though
I can still see both pictures quite clearly, I can't make out
whether they had facsimile signatures on them. It was obviously all the same to me.—I didn't admire these men for
their penmanship. I also sent away for a priceless book on
batting, a plain-cover no-nonsense paperback that looked
more like a French novel or possibly a work of pornogra-
phy. Naturally it had no date on it, but from the players
quoted in it I deduced that it came from the late teens or
early twenties; Jake Daubert and Zack Wheat of the Dodgers
were in there, along with Tris Speaker and lots of Ty Cobb
and dozens of others, conveying in bits and pieces, like
birds bringing twigs in their beaks, all the wisdom of the
dead-ball era—in particular all that there was to know
about place hitting, and all the good reasons for batting left-
handed. Since *Baseball* magazine was still shipping this
book out as hot copy in 1942, I have to suppose that this
was still the conventional wisdom that the current crop of
players had either absorbed or rejected as they were growing up, as their elders had continued to pass on what *they*
had learned as kids, and to hell with Babe Ruth, as the

Japanese would say. At any rate there wasn't a word in there that our own new coach Father Felix Pepin wouldn't have endorsed word for word, lively ball era or no.

"I'd rather have a guy hit four singles in a game than one home run," Father Felix would say ("But Father—you're talking about a guy hitting 1.000" is the answer, but Felix was dead by the time it occurred to me)—and this sentence is as good a way as any to introduce my new friend and co-conspirator of that winter, a fellow addict and deep-thinker who would have given all his sermons and retreats about baseball if they'd let him. Felix Pepin was a tiny man, as his name suggests, from the farthest corner of Maine, who was used to dreaming away the long silent winters of that region on a magic carpet made of baseballs, so we fell on each other with a glee that only hermits know. One baseball nut in an institution is a sorry, rather desperate object, but two is a happy crowd, and we fell to burbling right away about the past as fans will, no doubt generating that low excited hum you hear as you enter ballparks.

By further good luck, Father Felix's heyday as a fan covered the same years as the books I was reading. The school library at Delbarton had not really grown in yet. You'd see a forlorn cluster of books at one end of a shelf and then a space punctuated by a single book, held up by dust, and then maybe a flower pot—this is New Jersey impressionism —and an old pair of tennis shoes. As with a ship's library, the books seemed to be there simply because the monks had these shelves and you had to put something on them. Such was the sheer randomness in fact that I can't remember any of the titles because none of them reminded me of any of the others, except for a P. G. Wodehouse (*The Luck of the Bodkins*) standing next to a Dale Carnegie, and somewhere else a book allegedly by Lou Gehrig which would later get lost and replaced by another by Mickey Cochrane, "as told to" the father of a kid in our school, Michael Moran, who also wrote for *Baseball* magazine.

It helps me to gauge the difference between *ca.* ten and *ca.* twelve to realize that I hardly remember a word of the Gehrig book, whereas the Cochrane seems like an old friend. The word I *do* remember from Gehrig might be of use to Bill James if he's planning a supplement to his *Historical Abstract*. It seems that the Iron Horse couldn't buy a home run in Griffith Stadium, Washington, because his line drives could never quite make it over the right-field wall: since he could clear the fences in Shibe Park, Philadelphia, quite handily—four times in one game, in fact—the Griffith Stadium wall must have been monumental, worthy of an epic by the other Griffith, in fact, and Senator left-hand batters probably just gave up on it. The only way out of that park that Gehrig himself could suggest was to do it Ruth's way with elongated pop flies. The uppercuts the Babe applied to the ball could, I gathered, hoist it higher than half the airplanes in service at the time.

If I'd read the Gehrig book a year or two later—who knows, *maybe* a Yankee fan today? It could have been a close call at that because the Cochrane book did sell me on the Tigers, and make them my American League representative for years, after the A's had finally given up the ghost and after their remains had been shipped off to Oakland by way of Kansas City to be born again, California-style, in bright green Halloween costumes.

Although such long-distance courtships as mine with Detroit have a way of cooling off, I still consider the quintessential American League game to be Tigers *v.* Red Sox, as the National League one used to be Cubs *v.* Giants and is now Cubs *v.* Cards. The Tigers of the mid-thirties with Cochrane up, as they say in racing, as playing-manager had also been the last AL team to thumb its nose successfully at the lordly Yankees before the deluge, winning twice in a row in '34 and '35, and Cochrane–Moran's account of it became my Iliad for the winter of 1942–43—which was not so much later, grown-up time, than the events described, but a couple of historic eras later for me.

Anyone contemplating baseball history is likely to find himself collecting dynasties in this way—great teams from the past which seem to tell whole stories of rise and decline like mini-civilizations, and which make handy day-dream centers that you can move into for a few minutes as you might move into shade on a hot day, for rest and reflection. As a child, Robin Hood and his merry men were my team and Sherwood Forest was my stadium, and then at sixteen, the show would move to the Roman Forum where the guys would be Caesar, Pompey, and Crassus. But that year it was mid-depression Detroit, with revolution in the air and company goons busting skulls over at nearby Flint, and at the center, this curious oasis of good cheer and hope and sparkling white uniforms, the Tiger locker room, where the hottest question was whether Hank Greenberg would play ball on Yom Kippur, and the worst thing that could happen was the time pitcher Schoolboy Rowe went on radio and blurted out the immortal words "How'm I doing, Edna?"

The Cardinals who were waiting to take on Rowe and the Tigers in the World Series in 1934 would shortly give the poor man reason to hate every one of those words letter by letter, painting his ears with them everywhere he turned, and I only hope he didn't take it out on Edna when he got home to Texas that fall. The records show that he pitched through the noise about as well as could be expected, but that he was never quite as good again as he had been that year. And it's a safe bet that he never had quite as much fun either. "Edna—why did you have to be called *Edna?*"

I had already read in the good old *Saturday Evening Post* about the painful affliction known as rabbit ears, which begins with a slight reddening of the area but after a short while hurts like eczema every time you step on the field. As soon as the bench jockeys know you can hear them, the only cure is deafness—and even then they hold up signs. When the Cleveland Indians complained about their manager, Oscar Vitt, in 1940, the Yankees festooned their dugout with baby bottles, diapers, and other nursery items and "the Cleveland Cry-Babies," as they were hastily christened, lost one of the few pennants they had a real shot at; and in 1937, after Cochrane returned to the game from a nervous breakdown earlier that same year, these same dignified Yankees mimed insanity from the opposing dugout, gibbering and rolling their eyes and just conceivably distracting him from the pitch that ended his playing career for good that year. Bump Hadley threw Mickey an inside fastball and when Cochrane came to his senses the next day he had lost all interest in playing and all gift for managing; and soon afterwards one of baseball's fiercest competitors drifted listlessly out of the game for good, no doubt to concentrate on his writing.

But naturally, being twelve, I thought that bench-jockeying sounded like fun, and although I myself screamed like a demented rabbit at the slightest criticism, then and now, I was mysteriously sure that I would have no trouble with it. Since Father Felix was twelve too for all intents and purposes when we talked about baseball, he didn't disabuse me about this. But he did make one thing utterly clear to me, which was that serious baseball fans were primarily interested in the National League where the real game was played, and preferably (he didn't insist on this) they were not Dodgers fans. (It was true that once upon a time Tris Speaker, Duffy Lewis, and Harry Hooper had played for the Red Sox, and to the closed mind of Father Felix you could find no better baseball anywhere. But no doubt the breakup of this Olympian trio had broken his heart as definitively as the Dodgers leaving Brooklyn would bust mine and he gave no further shrift to the American League.) Purists like Felix had no end of trouble with Leo Durocher, and it was no use pointing out that Leo was really a throwback to the early, brawling days of baseball, when ballparks doubled as gambling parlors and physical intimidation was as much part of the game as freezing the baseballs overnight and tipping the bat with the catcher's mitt—two tricks sanctified by Connie Mack himself.

Never mind. It was a throwback in the wrong direction, and besides, time had softened the hard edges of the early days into a tableau of jolly brigands winking over their mustaches and blowing foam off their beer as they stuck the ball in your teeth or drew major blood with their spikes. Durocher was too real, and "right now," and in your face (a phrase he could have invented) to belong in this picture, and when he fought, it wasn't like a donnybrook at a county fair with all the boy-os joining in heartily, but more like a mugging in a back alley.

But leaving aside Durocher for a moment—how could I possibly root for a team called "dem Bums"? All the things that the world loved about the Dodgers—the Sym-phony, Hilda Chester's cowbell—were like a jazz band in church to Father Felix, but he knew that a fan's allegiance was sensitive terrain, at least as much so as religion and politics, and he approached it with the utmost delicacy. "I've always thought of you as more a New York Giants fan," he said slyly. And it's so obviously a compliment to be always thought of as *anything* that I thought for a second I'd look into it.

But really, what was to look into? The Giants had finished a distant third in 1942, which might have been a basis for talks, but that winter they were stripped of most of their major leaguers, and had to bump their way through 1943 using retreads like Dick Bartell and Billy Jurges alongside deeply flawed morning glories like Joe Orengo and Johnny Rucker. Timing is everything in these matters: if I had become a fan in 1951 instead of 1941, I'd conceivably be a Giant fan today. But in '43 when it was proposed to me, the Giants were in the process of somehow crawling under the Phillies and finishing a dead last in the league (unheard of for them), and after two years in Philadelphia, I'd had it with dead last. Like a slum kid, I felt life owed me something and from now on all I asked in return was unbroken success and happiness, silk pyjamas and caviar for the rest of it.

For a heartbreaking account of what life actually gave me instead, turn to the next chapter—if I can even bring myself to tell it. But the subject here is dynasties, and Father Felix's suggestion may have led eventually to one of my strangest ones. What that good man was obviously talking about was the past—in his heart he was no more hung up on Mickey Witek and Ace Adams than I was. And in looking at the past, allegiances blur agreeably. It is possible after all this time to root for the Saracens over the Crusaders without being a traitor, and in the foreshortened world of sports, it is quite acceptable to think fond thoughts of yesterday's enemy. Or at least I hope so, because over the next couple of years I read Frank Graham's essential book about the Dodgers but also a number of texts on the Giants, and while I found it easy and a pleasure to renew my vows to the present and future Dodgers, I also found myself quite bewitched by the New York Giants of the early twenties.

This had so much to do with the frame the picture was hung in that I wound up falling in love with the frame itself. If the Tigers were the depression, and the Yankees were the boom, the Giants of 1921–24 were the dawn of the jazz age —they were speakeasies and gangsters and chorus girls; they were the old New York of Diamond Jim Brady and Lillian Russell flowing abrasively into the new New York of Arnold Rothstein and Flo Ziegfeld and million-dollar prize-fights. And indeed, as if keeping time with the decade, John Muggsy McGraw started off with a bang—a bravura last hurrah that brought him four pennants in a row—and then petered out, leaving McGraw more than ready to retire in 1932 at a preternaturally old fifty-nine.

It wasn't just Muggsy that took my fancy, but all of them —Frankie Frisch and George "Highpockets" Kelly and young Bill Terry whom McGraw had to coax to leave Memphis, the home of the Memphis Chicks (players didn't have to go to the big leagues if they didn't want to in the pre–farm system era—witness Lefty O'Doul, "the man in the green suit," who passed his best years playing for the San Francisco Seals).

What seems obvious now is that a generation of New York sportswriters must have fallen in love with this team themselves and conveyed their passion intact to me and maybe others. In particular, every portrait I ever read of Ross Youngs, the doomed center fielder, seemed like an elegy to lost youth as such, the writer's own, and McGraw's, and everybody's. Youngs had been granted just enough time on earth to set the league on fire before dying at thirty of Bright's disease, and this, along with the death of Christy Mathewson a couple of years before, apparently aged Mc-Graw visibly. Like other good baseball men Muggsy worshipped talent with the ardor of a love poet, or of Emil Jannings panting after Marlene Dietrich in *The Blue Angel,* and the only reason Youngs's death didn't kill him on the spot was his discovery just before that of young Mel Ott.

As a faithful reader of a little-known publication called, I think, simply *Baseball Comics* (if it had baseball in the title, I read it), I already knew that McGraw had brought Ottie, as we drearily called him, to New York at age sixteen and wouldn't let him go again, for fear some bumbling minor-league manager might tinker with his style and let the magic talent escape. But only now as I write this do I see the obvious connection between this mother-hen concern and the slow dying of Youngs. Ten years earlier, McGraw *had* entrusted Youngs to a minor-league manager, with the words "Take good care of him, because if anything happens to him, I'll hold you responsible." Now he was taking no chances at all.

Since the sportswriters clearly had *not* lost their hearts to the historical Dodgers, neither did I, although you could hardly help liking them. In fact, this was my complaint: the Superbas, as they used to be called, seemed to have spent their first fifty years or so, before Durocher got there and used up all the credit, simply being likable, a buddy not a sweetheart, and this was something else that Philadelphia had spoiled me for, it being a town where the historic charm of Connie Mack had become positively the only selling point left for any of our teams. So I read about Nap Rucker and Dazzy Vance without catching fire, and about Van Lingle Mungo with positive irritation—were they *trying* to be cute, or what?

Of course, it was not they but the writers who were trying to be cute: you wrote serious about the Giants and funny about the Dodgers. But their images were good enough for me and, on the basis of those, I realized with a start that if I were transported back in time twenty years or so, I would probably find myself going along with Father Felix and rooting for the Giants, as described, after all—unless of course they were playing the Athletics of 1929, my unshakable all-time favorite dynasty (I wasn't *that* fickle). Now *there* was a team for you. If the Yankees of 1927 were the greatest of all time, then what did that make the team that, starting two years later, proceeded to beat them three times in a row by respectively 18, 16, and 13½ games? Scrapple?

Besides, the A's were still a presence. Lefty Grove had only just last year gone raging into private life after winning his 300th game in 1941, and Al Simmons, who coached intermittently for the A's, was about to unretire himself and embark on a quixotic wartime quest for his 3,000th hit. (All he succeeded in doing, besides reminding people of how old he really was, was to lower his lifetime average a few points—to .334!) Jimmy Dykes, the third baseman, was currently managing the White Sox, where he employed the rest of the old A's outfield, Mule Haas and Bing Miller, as his coaching staff.

But these men did not remind me of youth. Dykes was a spectacular example of an almost universal phenomenon back then: having retired from active sports, he had set to work removing any trace from his body that it had ever played anything. Once upon a time, I'd have said that Dykes wound up looking like a banker, but bankers look much better than that these days, and so do head waiters and food writers. In fact, future generations may find it hard to imagine how old and fat and out of shape baseball coaches of that era could manage to make themselves look from their late thirties on. If Miller Lite beer had existed back then, I doubt its advertisers could have rounded up a quorum that even understood the concept "less filling," let alone acted on it.

So if the A's still cast a shadow, it was a fat one, and it made their era, and all the eras, seem farther away than

ever, as if a twelve-year-old's time was the correct one. So
be it. It was time now for all ages to look at the calendar. In
February, Father Felix, who wanted no truck with this softball nonsense, actually tried hitting some ground balls to us
in the gym. Bad for the ball, bad for the floor, but intoxicat-
ing for us while it lasted, like a dip into an oxygen tank. The
ball bounced true on that surface, enabling me to backhand
a couple and develop on the spot a love affair with infield-
ing. (Later that spring, I would pick up a couple of royal
shiners, regular sunsets, from expecting real ground to be-
have so well. But the gym had taught me to keep my head
down, and I survived.)

Dynasties are for winter, when all baseball teams, past
and present, are equally becalmed. But by March, the living
are loosening up in Florida and Arizona, and it's time to
leave the study and start speculating on *future* history—
particularly on what Branch Rickey has in store for the
Dodgers in 1943.

For Father Felix spring meant something else as well. I
may so far have presented Felix Pepin as a rather narrow
man, interested only in baseball, but he had another side to
him. He also loved the horses. And most any time of the
year, if you found him with a big grin on his severely handsome face around suppertime, it meant his mind bets had
all come in that day at Hialeah or Hollywood Park or wherever, and he was a rich man, in his mind.

In those days, the New York *Daily Mirror* ran a comic
strip with captions written entirely in the form of disguised
racing tips, and Felix started each day decoding that between sips of his Breviary. After which, I don't know what
he did—where does a monk hide his racing forms? But he
claimed to come out ahead every year, and I'm sure he did.
If life had been a movie and he had turned out to be a
bookie in drag, it would not have seemed more unlikely

than the truth did. Because the one subject I can't remember ever talking to Father Felix about was religion.

But, as I would later learn just from looking at the box seats at major sports events, clerical sports nuts were as common as daisies in the old American church. So Father Felix was probably not the only priest to start pawing the ground come spring and flaring his nostrils. The tracks in the Northeast would be opening soon, and Felix Pepin's thoughts would begin to run to Monmouth Park, New Jersey, to which he would repair in black pants and a green school windbreaker and bet such dribs and drabs of money as the vow of poverty allowed him. But one day, before he could slide into the men's room to change into his threadbare disguise, an attendant accosted him in a scary voice with the words "Don't you go in there, Father!" "Why not? What's going on in there?" piped Felix, as a good straight man should, and the attendant wound up and unloaded his high hard one on him. "I seen a lot of priests go in there, Father, and I never seen one come out."

So. Spring. Father Felix. Baseball. What do you mean, there's a war going on?

6

The Pits

There was a war going on all right, and nobody knew it better than baseball fans. Although most of the shortages on the home front were a joke, and hardly enough to justify even the good-natured grumbling that the English had made so popular during the Blitz, the shortage of baseball talent was critical, and even more painfully noticeable than the substitution of phony meat in the frankfurters—a hot dog still looked like a hot dog and you could paint your margarine yellow, but there was no hiding that chunk of Spam you had playing shortstop or a pitching staff made of powdered eggs and instant milk. And the shortages remained as unfair as the black market itself. The youthful

Cards remained sufficiently intact, while the aging Dodgers fell apart; Pete Reiser went overseas, aching head and all, Stan Musial stayed home. And Branch Rickey only made it worse.

But to begin at the beginning. I lied when I said the teams went to Florida and Arizona that March. They did so only in my dreams. Otherwise they stayed right where they were in the Frozen North, ostentatiously saving gas and train seats and dashing my favorite winter dream, that of ballplayers limbering up under palm trees in places with exotic names like Orlando and Sarasota and Bradenton. Instead the Dodgers went up the river a few miles to Bear Mountain, and worked out in the West Point field house, which I assumed meant they were fielding ground balls off a gymnasium floor like the rest of us. It was worse than biting into a wartime hamburger.

After that fright, however, 1943 turned into a reasonable facsimile of a major-league season—1944 would be the real, four-star, triple-feature horror movie. But Branch Rickey couldn't wait. He saw no point in scrambling for the 1943 pennant. It was a season that would stand off by itself in baseball history anyway, like a peninsula—attached by a thread to the past, but unconnected to the future. You could build no dynasties in 1943, since half the team might be missing in action by the following year, but only squeeze one last drop out of whatever you had and wait to see what the post-war world would bring. And for Rickey, winning in '43 would have been doubly pointless, because it would have meant winning with another man's team—and grownups, I was learning fast, liked to have things all to themselves just as much as children do.

Of course, Rickey didn't let us in on any of this, so all we saw was this weirdo with the thick glasses and the fruity vocabulary tromping all over Larry MacPhail's beautiful sand castle, trading first Joe Medwick and then Dolph Camilli to the Giants, of all teams. Didn't this man know *anything?* Camilli at least attempted to set him straight by refusing to report in the most emphatic way possible: by retiring from baseball. "We really hated the Giants," he said—a line which struck me as the height of nobility at the time, though it slightly surprises me now. Do professional ballplayers hate? Apparently they did in those days.

With these two iniquitous deals went my dream of blending the old world with the new, the best of the lordly Dodgers with the cream of the whippersnapper Cardinals. Rickey only knew how to build one kind of team, a team of jackrabbits, and to hell with it. We wanted Larry MacPhail and his instant gratification and his whiskey tantrums back right now and not this corn-fed, psalm-quoting creep who didn't even know how you dressed for New York but decked himself out like the Arkansas traveler in a black coat and a totally unbelievable string tie.

However, even MacPhail was in the army, it was the place to be this year, and Rickey had just gotten the hint faster than we had. What the market did have to offer right now, aside from veterans on their last legs, was a profusion of kids of a kind that must have had Rickey's mouth watering, in a wholesome sort of way. And it helps me in forgiving the man posthumously for the lousy war he gave us to realize that among the children Rickey entertained during the Bear Mountain exile were the likes of Duke Snider and Gil Hodges (no jackrabbit—Rickey was looking for Dodgers not Cardinals) and that he had already cast a speculative eye on the Negro leagues and was figuring out how to work a Negro player onto his team after the war.

So he was out doing the Lord's work all along—but I can only say it didn't show. The couple of times I saw the Dodgers in '43, there were no young geniuses in sight,

although the old-timers whom war and Rickey had spared
so far, such as Billy Herman and Arky Vaughan, still sparkled
prettily. Whitlow Wyatt pitched a relaxed masterpiece one
Sunday in Philadelphia, a shutout with 22 outfield putouts I
could have caught myself, and I was sure we could have
given the Cards a run for their money if Rickey had left well
enough alone.

As it was, he cared so little for *anything* about 1943 that,
with second place still on the line, the Brooklyn starters
against the Phils for the last double-header between the
teams were, if memory serves, a couple of nobodies named
Hal Gregg and Rex Barney. Each of these would eke out
one fairly good year which would justify hiring them, but
on the whole Rickey was still firing blanks at this point—
and anyway, as noted, your sophisticated young fan wants
no truck with players he hasn't heard of before; like fight
promoters, we tend to snarl "Get yourself a reputation, kid,"
the minute they show up for auditions.

As for the A's and the Phillies, the comic relief in my
baseball life, there were only a few blips on the chart that
year—the Phillies had long since lost their only good
pitcher, Hugh Mulcahy, back in the winter of 1940, in the
same peacetime draft that made off with Hank Greenberg,
and the A's now lost theirs too, Phil Marchildon, at the end
of 1942. After that, there was nothing much for the draft to
take from us, it was like burgling an empty apartment, and
Philadelphia baseball became the greatest of all escapes
from the war, since our wartime teams looked exactly like
our peacetime ones. At a time when neighboring medioc-
rities like the St. Louis Browns and the Chicago Cubs were
seizing the opportunity to shinny up the pole while the big
boys were away, our guys were cementing their respective
holds on last place and playing hell with whatever passed
for morale in wartime Philadelphia.

Samuel Beckett could have written a good novel about the Athletics, to go with his *Murphy* and *Malone* series: called simply *McGillicuddy,* or possibly *Mack's Last Tape,* it would have described an ancient man sitting by himself on a dugout bench, too old and stubborn to move or even remember why he is there, muttering "I can't go on, I'll go on" to a crowd of bored reporters, while on alternate days, a bum with "Phillies" on his back stumps forlornly about the stage, knowing full well that if Godot ever does show up, he'll have to trade him immediately to pay for his supper that night.

The wartime Phils did manage one distinction—two future managers in the infield, count them, two, Bobby Bragan and Danny Murtaugh, both terrible ballplayers; and the A's had a distinction too—they surged as high as sixth in 1944 past a couple of sleeping forms, before returning to the servants' quarters in 1945.

By the time the World Series came round I had absorbed some of Branch Rickey's attitude toward 1943, and I listened with half an ear as the Yankees played the Cards once again. If the Cards won, great, but if they lost, that's 1943 for you. Their draft-dodgers were better than our draft-dodgers. And besides, I decided as the ship went down, sequels are never any good anyway.

Anyway, it was no skin off my nose—my family and I left Torresdale that fall in the direction of New York where the winners were, and not just in baseball. New York also had quite a respectable pro-football team, and before the year was out I would find myself sitting happily in the Polo Grounds watching the Giants making a game of it (a boring game, as was their wont, but you can't have everything) against the elite Green Bay Packers, featuring the great Don

Hutson. I have never to this day seen anything quite like Hutson, though Fred Biletnikoff with a pound of glue on each hand came close, and Michael Jordan in an allied sport is even better. On one particular play, the two armed guards who followed Hutson seemed to have him blocked out completely, so that either one of them had a good shot at the ball, and he had absolutely none. Yet somehow a pair of large hands inserted itself into the melee and made off with the jewelry. My father, who had been wallowing in his usual football illiteracy ("Anyone can run behind interference," indeed!), let out a gasp of pure, non-facetious admiration, while I could only wonder why, with so many dishonest ways to make a living, Hutson bothered with the rigors of football at all.

My father had already let out one other gasp that day, but it was a case of mistaken identity. On a triple reverse infinitely smoother than any of George Munger's "Hippopotami escaping from a swamp" variations at Penn, Don Hutson, who had not yet introduced himself, had hauled off and thrown a bomb of his own devising to another receiver who had sneaked as far past the competition as Secretariat one day would at Belmont, and we both marveled at *Hutson's* ability to get that clear—not to say his ability to hang on to such a wobbly pass. But what can you expect from a couple of Brits?

Hutson could do things like that, because he wore next to no padding in order to keep his arms free and by chance I would see him get his comeuppance later that fall on a trip to Philadelphia (dentist's visit) when he made the mistake of intercepting a pass and the whole Eagle team seemed to descend on him, like the French closing in on the Scarlet Pimpernel after years of frustration, and crush him to powder.

So move over Sammy Baugh, I had a new specimen for

my museum, a new type of human to study. If Baugh was the quintessential lean, twangy Texas Ranger, Don Hutson was Johnny Reb himself, one of General Lee's lieutenants maybe, skinny, curly-haired, happy-go-lucky—a cavalry officer who specialized in daylight raids behind enemy lines, now, fortunately for us, sublimating with football, like his whole region.

Baugh didn't have to move far though, because I saw him too at the Polo Grounds, and he was both more and less than I expected. For one thing, I don't think he threw a pass more than 25 yards all day, and I began to doubt whether he could, and for a single-wing tailback, he couldn't run for spit: in other words, he was a T-formation quarterback whose ship hadn't come in yet, and who was just trying to stay alive in the meantime. So he ran like an old lady who thinks she hears burglars. (There's nothing sexist about this: it's just my impression that old men prefer to hide in closets at such times.)

Those were the minuses. But on the plus side, nobody until Joe Montana came along would ever be as good at exploiting the short passing game as Slinging Sammy. As he zinged his line drives left and right for six, seven, eight yards a pop, the short pass began to look like one of those fundamentally unfair tactics, like the flying wedge, that upsets the normal balance between offense and defense and would have to be outlawed any day now.

But that was only when it was working. When it wasn't, Baugh's flips out to the flat could be juicily interceptible with not a soul in sight to disturb you afterwards. In fact, when it wasn't working you could lose 73–0 (though to be fair, Baugh was out for most of that game). It would not be until Montana came along that the short pass really *would* become unfair, as Baugh's improvisations gave way, after forty years of football evolution, to Bill Walsh's meticulous choreography, with the whole field covered in imaginary dance steps.

The other thing about Baugh was that the man could kick. Oh my, yes. Possibly to make up for his running deficiencies, Baugh had polished his punting to a high shine—so much so that his record for average distance still stands after generations of specialists have come and gone. It was, he may have felt, the least he could do. Most of today's players are only expected, like Isaiah Berlin's famous hedgehog, to know just one thing well, but yesterday's tailbacks were expected to pass at least five stiff tests and one optional one. Running, passing, blocking, tackling, and pass coverage were mandatory, and a failure in any one of them could count against your score in the others. Kicking was an extra, but highly valued, because the tailback alone was able to execute that nifty antique, the quick kick on third down. In fact, I saw Baugh get one off that very day, and unless memory fails more than usual, it was a beauty, 66 yards into the coffin corner. [Football record-keeping is notoriously sloppy, but I have a hunch that Baugh's distance record may have been padded slightly by quick kicks which were (a) initiated close to the line of scrimmage and (b) seldom if ever caught in flight. As I recall, this 66-yarder included a favorable bounce.]

The second time I saw Baugh that greedy season (it was a cinch to get to games in New York after my trial-by-trolley in Philadelphia) was no ordinary game. It was a playoff for the Eastern Division championship. And what was notable about it from my point of view was that I, a twelve-year-old boy on his own, had simply gone up to the ticket window, chewing and scratching, and gotten a reasonable seat. I never could have done that at the Army–Navy game, or even Penn–Cornell. Pro football in those pre-television days was a poor relation of the colleges, and if I thought being a baseball fan was a lonely calling outside the big-league cities, being a pro-football fan was downright eremitic. Lighthouse-keepers have more company. Beekeepers have more company.

So how did I get into it? Dr. Daley's enthusiasm, to begin with, which gave the impression of being part of a mass movement, although it was all coming from him. Then there was my father's gruff dictum, "I'd rather watch men play than boys." But mostly, it was my own doing. Whatever it is that makes your heart go ping or stand still or talk to the trees when you see a particular sport had happened to me with football on sight, even in its ramshackle wartime condition. I *liked* three yards and a cloud of dust. And the reason I chose the pros was the reason I choose the pros in any sport, which is not because they're better (with football the way it was played then, who could tell?) but because they hang around longer so you can get to know them. Your heroes have reached the top now and there's no place else for them to go. Except, of course, the army that year—and here football seemed to have a slight edge. All my guys, at least, had trick knees or obscure bones that hadn't knit properly, which still left them fit for sixty minutes both ways of killer football, but obviously in no shape for a desk job in the military. So although wartime football was also hell in its own way, it seemed a rock of stability next to baseball.

It is not quite true that it's out of sight, out of mind with me and football, but close. The last game of the season is always a sad thing. By the fourth quarter, the stadium is dark and cold as a morgue, and you know that the distant figures out there—they're always distant in football—have only signed on to entertain you for a few minutes longer, after which it's out into the winter you go. The players might as well be an orchestra playing on a sinking ship; neither their heart nor yours is really in it any more.

Still, it's nothing like as bad as baseball; you don't go around dressed in black for weeks afterwards or sob into your pillow. Every year I find myself missing the distinctive patterns of football for exactly three Sundays—the receivers flaring out from the line of scrimmage as the passer drops back, or the runner (let's call him Gale Sayers) slicing into the secondary and hip-faking the free safety out of his socks —but once they're gone they're gone. I wouldn't want to see them at any other time of year, and I know that next August I'll resent them as bitterly as ever as they try to cut prematurely into the baseball season once again.

Since it's a swell sport when it isn't competing with my wife, baseball, I'm delighted these days to see the pro season stretching as far as it can in the other direction until it practically touches the rim of major-league spring training. The free-fall into December used to seem pretty damn depressing, if only because it made you aware of winter for the first time. It was like being left off the trolley a mile before you've reached your stop, and I remember trudging home in the dark after the last game of some season, feeling lower than a Swedish playwright and wondering what it was all for. If your team had won, you got a little light and warmth from that. Otherwise, zilch, nada, the big nothing.

So you gather your baseball library around you and search for scraps of news about God's game in the paper— and you suddenly can't even find any football news. God, these people are fickle. What on earth do I care about ski reports from Vermont? Indoor track might have possibilities, though—my father surprises me by liking track, and we go to the Melrose games one winter, I can't remember which one, and he tells me all about Jack Lovelock, the New Zealander who won the 1500 meters in the Berlin Olympics in '36, looking back at his opponents so as not to beat them by any more than he had to. A lesson in chivalry which I have never had the least chance to use.

Throughout the war, the conquest of the four-minute mile became the track fan's own little V-Day, and I tried to get interested (it was sports, wasn't it?) as visiting Swedes and home-grown 4-Fs hurled themselves at it. But talk about watching paint dry and grass grow—the A's would be out of the cellar and Chuck Yeager would have outraced sound itself before this comparatively modest and totally arbitrary feat was accomplished. Sports does this from time to time: it barks out a number—.400, or 8.9 seconds, or 58 strokes —and everyone becomes transfixed by it as by a magic rune.

Anyway, it gave me something to root for until the box scores arrived—and so did what was left of the PGA golf tour, which remains to this day my ultimate winter thumb-sucker. Nowadays, I enjoy it as much for the sunny courses and the only kind of nature ramble I could ever stand, one with a ball in it, as for the game itself. But back then in my rag-picking days, it was for the sake of scores, any scores, attached to familiar names. At some point the next year, when I was laid up for a while, I even took to reading the racing results to see how many winners one T. Atkinson had ridden yesterday as opposed to E. Arcaro.

These tics and twitches, which must seem quite alarming to normal people such as mothers, are I believe common or garden symptoms of baseball withdrawal. Bear in mind that for six months of the year, we become used to real meat in the sports pages—Johnny Pesky going 3 for 4, Eddie Miller getting five assists and two putouts and, of course, no errors, good solid stuff like that—and then suddenly, the page goes blank except for Gunnar Thunderfoot breaking the 4.06 barrier and Byron Nelson shooting a 69: it's yet another form of Spam, but you've got to eat *something*.

Salvation that winter of 1943–44 came, though, from a quite unexpected new direction: I discovered the joys of competitive basketball, which has to be one of the all-time pleasant surprises of my sports life. Who could have guessed that this sloppy, time-killing activity of bounce, bounce, and shoot, and more bounce-bounce—marking time till summer—and more shoot could tighten up into something so incomparably dramatic?

Compared with baseball or football, basketball had never looked particularly theatrical—it seemed too improvised and harum-scarum, with people waving their arms and bumping into each other. But to be propelled from the bench into a tight game is as close to theater as sports gets. Even the boards underfoot feel the same, and the lights that set you off in bold relief from the ordinary world, and the sense that you are stepping onto a stage which can make you a star within minutes, or break your heart in less—or conceivably both. And it will have this power for you every time you go out there, you will never be safe, never have it made. Olivier could blow his lines even as he was bringing down the house, and Patrick Ewing can miss three foul shots in a row in the deciding seconds (or maybe not).

The differences are of course that you don't so much tread the boards as pound them to pulp and that you somehow have to contrive to write your own lines as you go, with somebody else's elbows in your face. You'll usually find that the coach's instructions hold up for about three seconds, or until you realize that the guy who's defending you isn't doing what he's supposed to and that it's a whole different world once you're in it—different *because* you're in it, and different because of the fundamental, non-negotiable difference between reality and conjecture. There is an element in every game that is invisible from outside, so that just as you could watch every moment of a love affair and still not know what they see in each other, so no spectator ever sees quite the game the player experiences.

My basketball immersion had two quick consequences, the first being that I said goodbye to snow forever. It was still handsome stuff, I suppose, so long as it didn't block the door of the gym, but the hard fact is that you don't play it with a ball, so that was that. The closest thing winter weather allowed in the way of a ball game was something you seemed to play mostly with your ankles and a ball that had been hammered flat. A French-Canadian kid blew into school just long enough to show us how a slap shot works (like a five-iron if you took a running start at it) and all we could see were his feet as they flashed over the ice. Never mind what he did with his hands—but you had to be born with those feet. So we seemed to give up hockey in a body, and obviously sledding is for small kids unless you plan to turn pro (whatever I thought that meant), so basketball wound up having a pretty big winter at the school. We had a new gym that year with fluorescent lights and enough heat to flood your hair with sweat on the first fast break. And if you were on the team, you entered the gym like a star on Oscar night.

The second consequence was my discovery that after a really good game, the kind that demands and takes all you have in you, I temporarily ceased being a fan of any team but the one I played on myself. I could replay that particular game over and over, up to a point, and plan for the next one, but I didn't give a damn how Seton Hall (our local team) did in whatever tournament it was playing in—or even how the Dodgers were going to do next year. And then finally, I wouldn't care how *we* did later either, but would be ready to change the subject. Possibly even to read something.

So the cure for sports, if you really want one, is more sports—but played instead of watched, because there is no such catharsis to be had on the sidelines, or on your sofa at home. The fan watching a game fills up with unrequited excitement, but all he can do about it is go back for more. And even downing game after game, he can't get rid of the thirst. The player gets it over with. His excitement has a natural end.

Although basketball is a much tenser game to play than baseball, neither in my small experience is half as tense as rooting. The basketball player, my kind at least, was much too busy running around stopping leaks, or turning on faucets that didn't work, for tension to build very much. *How did we let* that *happen? Why isn't this working the way it does in practice?* There is always something to do, something to keep you busy. And if you fail, that leaves you with something *else* to do for next time, more work for mother. The fan, meanwhile, can do nothing.

If you think I'm going out of my way at this point to avoid talking about the events of that summer, just consider how long it took Charles Dickens to get around to the death of Little Nell. The Dodgers in 1944 were more pathetic in my book than all of Dickens's heroines laid end to end. So just imagine (and here we turn up the organ music to Egyptian plague levels) coming all the way from Philadelphia to witness this mess: it was like going to a great restaurant and finding it had become a diner, or learning that the Parthenon now showed pornographic Westerns. Great deeds had been done in this place only yesterday by great men, but you would never guess it from the current inhabitants slumped on the front porch, either too old to move or too young to remember anything (when Babe Herman came back in '45 for a last obligatory trip over first base, he was old enough to have fathered at least half the numerous shortstops Rickey tried that year).

To look on the bright side, I was getting closer. I had arrived in Philly a good nine years after the last dynasty had pulled out. But this time, the sheets were still warm and the dishes were still in the sink. And, of course, the war would be over any day now, releasing all the great players in a magical body. I had listened to the news of D-Day on Father Felix's radio and had been vicariously liberating Europe ever since along with Papa Hemingway and Marlene Dietrich: with Paris falling so easily, we would surely have all the guys back in time for the pennant drive. If I'd known that Nazi generals were already tumbling over each other in Allen Dulles's waiting room in Zurich, trying to surrender to someone, I'd have wired the president to accept the next offer, or at least send us Billy Herman. The mood on the home front was so festive as we watched our horse come down the stretch that it is still hard to believe that the Battle of the Bulge and the discovery of Auschwitz were ahead of us.

Besides, Brooklyn was no place to feel mournful. Although strictly as a place to play baseball, Ebbets Field struck me then and now as a Little League version, if we'd had Little League back then, of Shibe Park, no bigger than a city apartment, with its puny dimensions and a stringy porous screen in right. Baseball wasn't the half of it in Brooklyn. This was preeminently a feel-good park, as opposed to the feel-like-slashing-your-wrists park I'd just left. The spanking blue seats gave your heart a lift on sight, and they seemed to have been gathered close to the field, the way people pull up their chairs to get a better look at something. And the connoisseur of baseball sounds might have picked up the quaint impression that the fans actually seemed to be talking to each other and not just issuing stray grunts and unidentified noises to no one in particular. These people were in fact formidably capable of entertaining themselves—though if someone felt like playing a little baseball today, that was fine too.

Ebbets Field was the real civic center of Brooklyn, and in that respect I had caught it at a happy time. All war long, the borough had been falling steadily more head over heels in love with itself, egged on by an amused nation. The other characters in the war movie might be an Oklahoman or a Texan, an Alabaman or a Mississippian, an Ohian or an Indianan—in any event, the representative of a vast region, South or Midwest, or Far West, with each state getting its quota—except for this one crazy guy who just wants to know "how da Dodgers are doin' " and by so saying makes this clutch of marines or sailors or frogmen a quintessential American gang. The Brooklyn guy was like a mixer on the bar that goes with absolutely everything and turns it into a red, white, and blue cocktail.

Like many things—the big bands for instance—this fabulous concoction did not outlast the war by much. And it ended for good in 1958 when the diabolical Walter O'Malley stripped the borough of its identifying symbol, its flag and its rallying point, and shipped da Dodgers off to Los Angeles where American myths go to die, though usually not while they're still alive and kicking. But in 1944 none of this was in view, and Brooklynites expected nothing but roses from the future, which would begin any day now, without warning, with Pee Wee Reese standing at short and Reiser back in center and everything right with the world.

137

So it turned into a goofy good-natured season after all—not what I had bargained for, but things were tough all over and we were all in the same boat. To make an old Yankee fan flinch, you have only to whisper the names Ossie Grimes and Mike Milosovich in his ear (although Tim Burke, that incomparable judge of talent, might have snapped up these same guys in peacetime too); with a Giant fan try Hank Luby or "Nap" Reyes. The Germans were rumored to be drafting everyone who could walk and see across the room, so I guess the Dodgers were lucky to be Americans and allowed to keep Eddie Bazinski and Howie Schultz, who could easily do both. It would have been downright unpatriotic to have a good team that year—in which case Brooklyn deserved a congressional medal for its seventh-place finish (all the patriotism in the world couldn't have gotten us underneath Philadelphia, the home of Liberty).

As with 1943, I think we could have done better, if Rickey hadn't chosen the moment to fulfill an obvious lifetime ambition to give every kid in America a chance to play in the big leagues for fifteen minutes. We did have a big-league outfield and, perhaps because he knew he had Duke Snider and Carl Furillo in the wings (and perhaps because he didn't want to be lynched after the Camilli and Medwick disasters), Rickey let them play every day without interruption by small fry.

But meanwhile the three major-league outfielders Rickey allowed to play, Dixie Walker, Goody Rosen, and Angie Galan, could only look on dyspeptically while Rickey's Kids tried their growing hands at the two positions every kid would want to play for his fifteen minutes, pitcher and shortstop, which are, by ill chance, kind of important in baseball.

Fortunately, this was at least a losing team that declared itself early, so there was no unnecessary suffering. The first time we played the Giants in April, they beat us 26–8, with a retread named Phil Weintraub driving in 11 runs that day (even their retreads were better than our retreads) and I heard every pitch of the massacre on Father Felix's radio. And in case I missed the point, the Dodgers threw in a losing streak of 15 games in late June and early July, which was like a bell warning us all off the boat while there was still plenty of season to enjoy. Durocher himself seemed to abandon interest during the streak, barely bothering to show up at the park or smother his yawns: his many real gifts as a manager did not include babysitting, or the patience it takes to coax a seventh-place team into maybe sixth. Like everyone else, Leo had his eye on the end of the war—little guessing that it had its eye on him too and was preparing a swell practical joke for him. Maybe if he'd known how little time he had left in Brooklyn he might have tried to enjoy himself a little bit more that year. Because by the time the good players finally did come back and win the pennant Rickey had promised, the Lip was nowhere in sight or sound.

As every Cub fan knows, a losing team in a winning city can be quite endurable, even positively charming. And just walking from the subway to the ballpark past the Botanical Gardens reminded one of what an elegant, mellow old city Brooklyn was in those days. The jokes which made it sound like a saloon attached to a bowling alley in no way prepared you for the range and variety of the architecture or the populace. No two neighborhoods were exactly alike, and I'll swear that in no American city did you ever hear so many musical instruments being practiced behind so many windows. Yet even today, young maestros are known to say

WILFRID SHEED

"Can you imagine a little kid from Brooklyn leading the New York Symphony Orchestra [or whatever]." In truth, it's the least I'd expect from him.

The approaches to the other New York ballparks were nothing like so salubrious, but gave one instead a hint of the urban wasteland that peace would someday bring (another of history's jokes), but anything looks good on the way to a ballpark and I would give anything to be strolling once again with my friends over the improbable viaduct that leads from the West side of Manhattan to the Polo Grounds, in order to watch the Giants play one more game of baseball in their natural habitat. With the pennant races called off that year for all the local teams—although the Yanks made a mild run for it out of habit—we took turns visiting each other's parks and making fun of our own teams. "Mike Garback!" somebody would pipe. "No, no. Danny Gardella!" "Yeah? Well how about Calvin Coolidge McLish?" Some of these guys, like McLish, would actually go on to be pretty good, but they all sounded funny to us, simply because we'd never heard of them before.

Nineteen forty-four was the year we all learned irony, the ultimate irony being, of course, the success of the St. Louis Browns in the AL pennant race, which took all our teams off the hook. Now we *knew* the year was a joke. The only way the Browns could possibly top this joke was by playing a one-armed outfielder the next year—but it wasn't as funny. And later Bill Veeck would try a midget as well. (To the non-jock sensibility, both these gimmicks may seem prehistorically coarse and unfeeling. But Bill Veeck, who thought up the midget, was no stranger to affliction himself. Part of one of his legs was missing and his chapter on the subject in *Veeck—As in Wreck* was entitled "I'm not handicapped—I'm a cripple." He was a blunt and funny man, and if he thought it would get laughs, and sell tickets, he would have played himself.) But nothing came close on the laugh meter to the pennant in 1944, because that was a pure *baseball* joke. The Browns! The pennant! It's too priceless. We laughed till the tears ran. And kept laughing through the World Series when the Browns actually won two games, either because the Cards were also laughing too hard or because they had finally become a wartime team themselves.

That was 1944 for you. As the Allies seemed to waltz through the vaunted German army (although what was taking them so long? those looked like tiny countries) *everything* made us laugh. Particularly my first sight of the Polo Grounds in its baseball manifestation. Who in the world were they trying to kid? This was a *football* stadium, anyone could see that. You mean they're actually going to try to play baseball in here?

There must be some mistake. It's an iron law of American sports that you can't play baseball in a football stadium or vice versa, because the two sports are a different shape. A real ballpark trying to make like a football one has to put in extra seats in front of the regular ones, producing a patchy, amateurish look and a lot of second-rate seating; a football field dressed up for baseball is a gawky-looking joke, like a kid who's outgrown his clothes. The foul poles at the Polo Grounds were so close to home plate that if you sat next to one, you actually had a better seat than if you sat directly behind first or third. Meanwhile center field stretched to infinity—so that if you had a seat out *there* you would have had exactly four chances in the park's entire history to catch a fly ball.

Ridiculous—and all the more so as the Giants' wartime shavetails took turns hitting chip shots, like that feeble little thing Bobby Thomson would hit a few years later that they made so much fuss over, just over the railings. It seemed to me to give the team an unbeatable home court advantage, as I explained to my amiable new grown-up neighbor, Mr. Bob Kennedy, a Giant fan. If you play .700 ball at home, which should be a cinch in that park, you only have to play .500 on the road and you're in.

Naturally, I only remember my own lines, but Mr. Kennedy probably pointed out that .500 on the road isn't that easy for anyone, let alone a team designed to play in only one ballpark. True enough. For instance, that season Mel Ott, who had programmed himself to crank every manner of pitch around to dead right, got all but two of his 26 home runs at home, and I'm not sure he ever hit one out of Crosley Field, Cincinnati, where the foul lines were long but center field was no more than a three-iron from home plate.

So I entered the Polo Grounds with my sneer already in place, all set to discount any bad thing that happened, even a couple of shots by the new Giant, old sleeping beauty himself, Ernie Lombardi, that threatened to cave in the roof (they would have curled foul in another 100 feet or so, I decided).

But then I came across something in *Baseball* magazine —still the closest thing I knew to a scholarly journal—that wiped the sneer off my face. Babe Ruth was quoted as claiming that the best baseball was played at the Polo Grounds, because the pitcher had to work the corners there, he couldn't get sloppy and hope for the best—and I think he also said that the outfielders didn't have to run as far, which takes some of the authority out of the quote. The Babe would presumably endorse any park that allowed him to rest his feet a bit and take the load off his matchstick ankles. Then too, Ruth may have felt he owed the Polo Grounds something since it was there that he launched his second career as a home run hitter, before the Yankees had gotten round to devising a park even better suited to his requirements. It's a good question to chew on for a lifetime or so: how many home runs Ruth would have hit if he'd stayed at Fenway instead of getting his tailor to run up a stadium expressly for him. (Old-timers say just about the same number. But I doubt it. In 1919, Ruth hit nine at Fenway and 20 on the road. In 1920, he hit 29 at the Polo Grounds and 25 on the road. Ruth's swing was quite compact and judicious and, legend aside, he didn't hit as many tape-measure jobs as either Foxx or Mantle.)

Over against these small-minded quibbles we have, though, the fact that Ruth never said anything silly about baseball. Clown or no clown, he was deadly serious about this one thing, and played the game quite flawlessly, which means with total concentration. For all that's been written about him, there is no record of a mistake.

And besides, I liked his point. It occurred to me that if you could pitch well at the Polo Grounds, guarding the foul lines, but also at Crosley Field, preventing fly balls from straying too far to center, you were a complete pitcher. No such stark test exists today, although being able to pitch at Fenway Park and *anywhere* else comes close; pitching in Atlanta on either a dry or a humid night—the experts seem to differ—or in Wrigley Field with the wind blowing out also keeps a pitcher honest these days, but it doesn't require the smorgasbord of adjustments the old parks did: just check the number of triples hit in Forbes Field, Pittsburgh, versus the doubles in Sportsman Park, St. Louis, and you'll see what I mean.

So far, I had traded down in stadiums since leaving Philadelphia. Ebbets Field and the Polo Grounds were superior places to visit, with much better dialogue, but the exigencies of big-city real estate had left Ebbets no room to breathe and had squeezed the Polo Grounds into the shape of a lozenge. However, I have left out the equalizer. The Big Fellow, Yankee Stadium itself. Father Felix had taken a bunch of us into New York to watch the inevitable St. Louis Browns in 1943, and the first sight of that curious fringe on the roof absolutely knocked me out. Never mind the "House that Ruth Built" glamour—this was a majestic edifice even if you'd never heard of it before. The upper deck, as I would later learn when I had to limp to the top (don't ever try it on crutches), was banked extra steep and tall so that you seemed to be climbing to the sky in order to watch the game with Jupiter himself. And every girder seemed to proclaim, this is a house of champions, this is where the King lives.

The King happened to be in exile right now—the navy had grabbed DiMaggio between injuries—but this was clearly where he belonged, and it was entirely proper to the setting that when he was finished with his earthly duties a few years later he would hand over his crown to another King with a weirdly appropriate name, who would reign over the House of Ruth until it was finally brought low in the mid-sixties.

However, there was no one remotely like Mantle or DiMaggio on the wartime Yankees, and the stadium had to get by, like the Tower of London, strictly on its looks and its reputation, for those two grotesque years. I can only say that it was still a magnificent place to be, well worthy of my undying hatred. To be sure, the dimensions were kind of peculiar, with those ditzy little foul lines, but all was forgiven as the stands flared swiftly out and away into that opulent center field, with its famous Death Valley to the left and enough room for a triple to the right. There was nothing cramped or mean or pinchpenny about this place—

nothing that would drive a team to California, say—and its overall authority was such that if that's where the foul lines were, that was where they should be.

The summer of 1944 was one of those epic scorchers that still comes up occasionally when the talk turns to heat waves. Even Riverside Drive was hot that year. In fact, our apartment felt like the boiler room of a steamer passing through the Red Sea. But I could always cool off with base-ball—either watching it at one of the three great adult play-grounds, or playing it myself between police busts in the park immediately below us (picture a red-faced cop, loosely based on Edgar Kennedy of the movies, running us off every two weeks or so: he hadn't joined the police force for *this*). Baseball is cool communication whatever Marshall McLuhan says about it, but when even *it* boiled over, we would line up at the tepid water cooler, jamming our faces into the dribble, and then, if we knew our onions, spitting most of it out again: it was pop science gospel in those days that you mustn't drink much water when you were hot.

Then on Sundays a couple or a bunch of us would go off and *really* cool off at the ballpark. If you've got three big-league teams to choose from, one or more of them is always at home, and admission was cheap to all of them, and if you arrived early you were almost guaranteed a great seat, even if you were only thirteen. I understand that this must seem like science fiction to younger readers, but after three years of Sunday double-headers, I still had never been subjected to a seat in the sun or in back of a pillar or any place seriously distant from first or third.

And so what if the baseball was lousy? We could still watch Dixie Walker hunched over like a scientist delicately slicing his way to the batting title, and Stan Musial, mysteri-ously spared from the wars so far, lashing hellacious line drives off the Ebbets Field scoreboard in batting practice,

and Mel Ott yanking those 260-foot screamers of his into
the Polo Grounds seats. And we had the ballparks themselves, three historic sites in one city with as much history
roiling around each of them as any Civil War battlefield.
Whatever part anatomy may play in the lives of people, it
was undoubtedly destiny for ballparks in that pre-plasticene
era, and you could almost deduce the history of the three
local clubs and the very style and shape of their heroes just
from contemplating their workshops—even while the ap-
prentices were mucking about in them.

But the other reason for my relative detachment from the
pennant races of 1944 was probably less philosophical and
more muscular and neurological than the above. The truth
is, I was playing so much ball myself that year, from late
morning to sundown, that the principle first discovered in
basketball last winter of shrinking focus and diminishing
outside concern came into full effect, and the Dodgers
could fly a kite for most of the time as far as yours truly was
concerned.

Whether a Dodger pennant would have brought back the
old intensity is an interesting question: it would be nice to
think that one could have the best of both worlds—excitement in victory, indifference in defeat; it would make a nice
change from the usual law of life which decrees that defeat
always feels worse than victory feels good. (Or am I alone
in this? Defeat seems so solid and inarguable; victory is
comparatively elusive and hard to concentrate on. "I expect
this will hit me tomorrow" says the winning athlete. Defeat
never waits that long.)

Anyway, I'll never know for sure because that winter my
athletic career hit a snag at just the same moment as the war
did: the Battle of the Bulge actually occurred while I was in
the hospital fighting my own mini-battle with polio—a disease that, like the war, was supposed to be over by fall, and

which threatened now to lock me into being a pure spectator at a time when I might conceivably have escaped into
being a semi-pure player. My illness was no great tragedy
then, and it is certainly no tragedy now—nothing you can
get a novel out of is a tragedy—but artistically speaking it
forms a natural bracket, or bookend, around my tryst with
wartime baseball, and it did present me at the time with an
interesting question vis-à-vis the subject of sports in general:
namely, do you still want to go on with this? Are baseball
and football really that good?

Fate had given me a dandy excuse to change my life and
maybe start a new one as a wheelchair poet or egghead. For
all the deaths and rebirths I'd run through, I had *still* only
been a fan for four years at that point, so it was not too late
to consider the whole thing an episode, a love affair that
didn't pan out. ("Lord Chatterley, why not face the facts, my
dear.") To put it another way, did I really want to go on
talking to an old baseball glove for the rest of my life?

It would, as I say, have been an interesting question if it
had ever occurred to me.

7

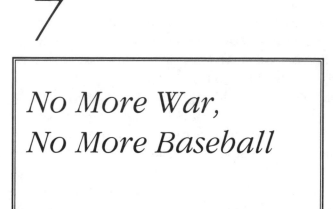

*No More War,
No More Baseball*

In my novel, the hero turns his back on sports with a snarl when he gets polio—but that's one of the reasons one writes novels: to see what was behind that door or down that road. My character, Brian Casey, was a man of action, not to mention a better athlete than I. But more significantly, he also had a much worse case than I did, which altered the whole equation.

Polio might best be described as a lifelong morning after or mopping-up operation. The disease hits like the Luftwaffe and you have one hell of a night or week, you're not sure which, and when calmness finally returns you crawl around the ruins checking what was hit and who's missing, and what seems miraculously to have escaped damage. But even while you're doing this, you're already at work rebuilding, pumping muscles that seem half-shot back to life and learning how to make a *gluteus maximus* do the job of an *anterior tibia*. The muscles I'd been building and overworking all summer on the ball field suddenly found themselves in straitened circumstances and fighting for their lives: but being an athlete certainly helps, as it helped FDR. And by the next summer I found that I could still swing a bat and throw a ball reasonably hard, albeit sitting down. And this discovery undoubtedly made all the difference between me and Casey, and Clifford Chatterley too, if you allow for our different interests.

And speaking of interests—at such a time, you are not usually trying to shed any of these at all, but if possible trying to multiply them to infinity. Your problem now is how to cope with all the blank time on your hands that hospitals are uniquely equipped to provide, like a roll of white canvas that keeps being replaced with more until you have quite enough to house every interest you ever had, with time left over to start a new life as well.

And what a new life it was at first. "Don McNeil's Breakfast Club," "Breakfast at Sardi's," "Breakfast with Ed and Pegeen"—enough breakfasts to stun an ox—followed by "John's Other Wife," "One Man's Family," Cliff Edwards as Jiminy Cricket, and that's it for me. "I'm not going to take it any more!"—with enough hours left over after you've snapped off the radio to read a whole Agatha Christie before lights out. It would have taken a more dedicated soul than mine to say during such a day "I'm turning my back on baseball now" or "Don't bother to bring me the Monday sports section with the pro-football scores this week. I'd rather stare at the wall a while longer and play another tune on the sheets with my fingers."

But sports did more than kill time in the hospital: they also fit nicely into your escape fantasies. In the heyday of polio, there must have been at least as many miracle cures in the air as there were sick people, and since you usually do get a little better as you go along, it didn't take outrageous gullibility to believe that you were going to go all the way someday—and where else to go than back to the ball field? The other kid in the emergency room walked out of there looking great after two weeks; okay, you rat—I'll be right behind you. The way I figured it was that I would just turn up at one of the real ball fields down by the river and start playing one day, without a word. No fuss, boys—let's just play some ball around here. But, hey! all *right*.

Wide awake, I never quite got that far. But by next summer I was pumping line drives out of my wheelchair, and by the year after that I could stand with a brace and snap a bat—or a Ping-Pong paddle, or a seven-iron—with tentative authority, just well enough to remember what it felt like and what the players were doing out there. And that was a good enough arrangement to be going on with—with one lingering exception, which I mention in case any reader thinks polio sounds so good he wants to rush out and get some. Watching professionals play remained an unbroken pleasure, and I was off to the ballpark that summer as fast as my crutches would carry me, whacking strangers in the shin as a form of crowd control. But it wasn't until my own late forties that I could watch amateurs of my own age play without thinking, *I* could do it better than that, you klutz, and getting almost too sore about it to watch.

So no adjustment is perfect, but this would do, especially in that sedentary, pre-exercise era, when half the guys I knew retired to their armchairs while they were still in their teens. Just walking to the ballpark, I actually had an edge on my friends that year, because you can really swing along on crutches, like Tarzan using underhand vines, and keep doing it as long as your hands hold out.

Last summer, I had gotten my kicks simply meeting the New York ballparks; this year I got them even more simply by just getting to the ballparks. But it was a kicky year in general, and I don't suppose the whole country has ever before or since felt so good from coast to coast and from ear to ear as it did in the summer of '45. In May, the strip-tease in Europe finally ended and the Germans said "uncle" unconditionally; and then, by the time the celebration of that had died down a little, the Japanese quit too, and the roof came off completely.

To be sure, the newsreels showed, between victory pictures, the first films of the death camps with the bones piled to the sky and finally our first glimpse of the mushroom cloud which still sits like a punctuation mark between that era and all future ones. It was, in sober fact, a terrible year. But nothing could wipe the goofy grin off Uncle Sam's face all that summer, or the cream off his whiskers. This was it, baby, this was what it was all about.

Since I had started the war two years earlier than my American friends had, I may have thought between V-E and V-J days that it was a little more thoroughly over than they did—but you couldn't tell it from the shit-eating expressions they all wore. So where were the ballplayers? Watching major-league baseball that summer was like sitting in the theater waiting for the play to start. First one member of the cast appears, to wild applause, and then another and then a long pause—but you don't mind waiting because it's going to be such a great play when it gets here and meanwhile the theater looks lovely tonight, and the ushers are friendly for a change and everyone seems to be in a good mood and the truth is you'd be happy to sit here forever.

In other words, we had another year on our hands when

winning a pennant wasn't strictly necessary—isn't winning the greatest war in history enough for you? If ever a summer signaled that there was more to life than baseball it was this one, and even I wavered for a moment or two before deciding to table the question till fall.

The Dodgers, in this laughing situation, probably played about as well in '45 as they should have the year before if they hadn't crapped around so much, and if Mr. Rickey hadn't tried to turn Ebbets Field into a summer camp. The wartime Dodgers were, in five words or less, a solid third-place team, which you arrived at by taking the difference between a first-place offense and a sixth-place pitching staff. But watch this kid Tommy Seats (remember him?) and maybe Ralph Branca. And above all, wait till next year.

As if to emphasize the comic opera side of the season, the draft finally seized on Stan Musial, presumably for police duty in Japan. This mysterious move probably tipped the balance just enough for the Cubs to win the pennant—but this was not funny the way the St. Louis Browns' pennant had been funny. The Cubs often won pennants in those days, and that particular one is only a joke in retrospect. (What would have been funny even then is if they'd won the World Series.)

So, okay, anything but the Cardinals, who were beginning to turn into the Yankees with their string of ho-hum wartime pennants: from rebel to fatcat in three easy seasons. The Cubs for their part were nice old gentlemen—Phil Cavarretta and Stan Hack must be a thousand by now—so they were no threat for next year, but more like some old dynasty having a last fling. "Hapsburg Summer," we'll call it. And I liked their uniforms—the sleeves were a different color (blue) than the rest of the ensemble. Very cheerful and about as threatening as the Vatican Palace Guards. So let them have their year in the sun.

By the luck of the draw, my friends seemed to lean toward the Bronx teams that year, and I probably watched
more Yankee games than anything else. This was fine too
(*find* me a cloud that year—I dare you), because the Stadium is a swell place to celebrate and because the American
League was having a pretty good pennant race and they
seemed to be conducting it over the dead bodies of the
Yanks.

My old friends the Tigers were having it out with the
Senators, who were *sort* of a joke, halfway between the
Browns and the Cubs: they had no future, but they did have
a scrapbook worth a few dollars. Pennants in '24, '25, and
'33—not bad considering those were the Ruth years and
the Foxxgrove years in Philadelphia. And Ossie Bluege, the
third baseman of those teams, was managing now. It was an
appropriate team to win in 1945, if no other time. Cubs–
Senators had a nice traditional ring to it for ringing out the
old, pre-war world. And next year, we could do the whole
thing properly.

But the Tigers were the story that year, the kind of team
that crosses the line into general-interest magazines. Hank
Greenberg had finally been let out of the service for a tan-
talizing taste of wartime pitching, which he gobbled up
according to plan (other veterans, such as my guy Cecil
Travis of the Senators, or Pete Reiser next year, did not
perform so obediently: our dream of a great post-war get-
ting-up morning had sat on the stove a mite too long). But
the hot news out of Detroit was the pitching, specifically
Hal Newhouser and Dizzy Trout—who got into the stories
partly because of his name but mostly because of his talent
—and then at the last minute, Virgil Trucks, another name
and another talent who turned up like the masked crusader
to clinch the pennant on the last day of the season.

My friends and I traipsed over to the Stadium one Sunday

153

in late summer hoping to catch at least one of the hot-ticket
Tigers and I can still see Hal Newhouser vaulting jauntily
over the bull-pen fence just in time to give us a peek and
incidentally to save the second game. Fireballing relief
pitchers went heavily against the grain of current baseball
theory, because they led to fly balls, wild pitches, and premature sore arms—and no double plays—but this was a
pennant race, so Newhouser was grudgingly allowed to give
us a sneak preview of what Joe Page and Goose Gossage
would later make a regular event at the Stadium: he just
blew the hitters away.

Like Sandy Koufax, Newhouser seemed to have had a
hinge loosened in his shoulder allowing his arm to whip
over his head at supersonic speeds—in fact he seemed to
have had several hinges loosened and appeared from the
grandstand to be a loose-limbed, loosey-goosey guy, with a
ferocious expression on his face. Subsequently, I would
watch Bob Feller, who looked as if he was shelling peas
from this same distance, and Robin Roberts, whose motion
was so deceptively smooth that he could have been pitching
from a rocking chair, and I can only report that Newhouser
looked as if he was throwing harder than either of them.
What the ball looked like is obviously another story.

The Yankees' only serious contribution to the pennant
race that year, other than either (1) rolling over like
whipped dogs for their opponents (a Dodger fan's view) or
(2) stepping aside and letting one of the little kids have it
(the Yankee fan's version), had turned out by then to be
more of a contribution to the *National* League pennant
race. In a move so bizarre that the Stadium stands buzzed
for weeks afterwards with talk of collusion, hanky-panky,
and downright insanity, the Yankees traded their one certified ace Hank Borowy to the Chicago Cubs, for whom he

would win eleven games to go with the ten he'd won for the Yanks and give him the best season in baseball.

Borowy also did his damnedest to make the World Series interesting, contriving to win two games and lose two in a fever of activity, before fading into the long twilight of the suspect-armed which the Yankees had probably envisaged for him a year too soon. It must have been a neat summer for Borowy, firing goose-eggs at batters and figurative ones at his ex-employers: but nobody, least of all the Yankees, was really looking at 1945 by then.

The 1945 World Series was the last World Series I would have to follow entirely on radio, but that wasn't the only thing that made it seem elegiac. If Cubs–Senators would have been an acceptably traditional matchup, Cubs–Tigers took you right into the bowels of history. The Cubs had actually won their last two championships against Detroit in 1907 and 1908, right after ballplayers stopped pitching underhand and pressing their pants sideways. Then in 1935, Mickey Cochrane's Tigers and mine had settled scores— and here were some of the same players, the boys of '35, on hand for this one: Hack and Cavaretta and Lon Warneke for the Cubs and Greenberg and Tommy Bridges for Detroit, taking one last curtain call on the big stage.

And these were not the only old-timers the teams had rounded up for this reprise of the thirties: sharp eyes could also detect Paul Derringer and Claude Passeau, Roy Cullenbine and the great Doc Cramer and the ultimate old-timer's old-timer, one Chuck Hostetler, who'd made his big-league debut just the year before at age forty-one—all taking their bows before the house lights go down for good on baseball's greatest era, and incidentally on my own childhood.

The quintessential play of that Series is actually two plays run together: I can still picture them as one through the scrim of a radio. Young Andy Pafko is feverishly searching for the ball in the Wrigley Field vines, while 300 feet away Chuck Hostetler, running like Father Time himself, stumbles rounding third and can't go on. Everything is frozen. The effect of this when you can only hear it is unearthly. What kind of prehistoric ballpark has vines in it for godsake? No time to find out now, but I can see them all right; thick and venomous with Pafko desperately plunging his hand in past snakes and the skulls of former left fielders, as the old man in the distance rises, staggers a few steps, and falls again, like Victor McLaglen riddled with bullets in *The Informer.* I'm sorry for your trouble, Chuck Hostetler, and all of you, but it was a grand hurrah you and the boys put on for us.

Never has the country enjoyed a World Series more or had a better sense of proportion about one. In the glow of victory, baseball seemed simultaneously precious and insignificant. It was one of those things we were fighting for— even people who'd never much liked the game seemed to agree on that (the post-war crowds would be swollen by temporary enthusiasts, who'd forgotten how boring baseball can be). But.

On the other hand, we had the Bomb now, we had the power to destroy everything on earth, baseball included— and what earthly reason did we have, with the reports just coming in from Auschwitz and the dust settling slowly and poisonously on Hiroshima and Nagasaki, to suppose we, or somebody like us, wouldn't use it someday? No one since has ever been as scared by nuclear weapons as we were those first few months, as Uncle Sam, the least likely suspect, stood there with the smoking gun in his hand.

It created the kind of mood in which you get out old photographs and look at them blankly, or decide to take in a ball game and can't remember the score afterwards. We felt good—we felt *great* in fact. But we were a little bit out of our depth right now. Tomorrow, as the winners say, it would probably all sink in.

If the year 1945 had been planned to wean me away from baseball, I can only say it did the best it could. That March I had gone to the polio spa and miracle farm in Warm Springs, Georgia—where I thought mainly about baseball; and in April, soon after I'd returned home disillusioned by Warm Springs, President Roosevelt had gone there too and died, which for kids of my age was like watching a face fall off Mount Rushmore. Unthinkable. "The Big Three is now the Big Two and a Half," I wrote someone, giving the anonymous Mr. Truman the biggest fraction I possibly could. But even at that dark moment, my mind probably strayed, this being April, to FDR's famous green light, which seemed to be stuck permanently on amber, as the bureaucracy wrestled with the problem of mustering a couple of hundred ballplayers out of the service.

Then that August, my sister and I had gone to stay with the Kennedys in Altamont, New York, well out of range of the Stadium and practically out of range of Red Barber, who sounded like a French resistance fighter from Alabama coming in on shortwave radio, and to compensate I discovered Graham Greene and some swell countryside. But to compensate for *that,* I also discovered the other Graham, Frank, and I wolfed down his book on the Dodgers even more greedily, along with J. Roy Stockton's book on the Cards. And if I had to boil that part of the summer down to one memory, it would not be of *Ministry of Fear* or *This Gun for Hire,* but of myself poking a line drive through the window of the Kennedys' living room after swearing I wouldn't. Rehab is rehab, but enough is also enough, and I thought Mr. Kennedy was going to kill me that night.

So my weaning was not going to be easy. Nevertheless it absolutely had to be done, because the end of the war marked the end of our reason for being here, and we were off to England in the spring, where no baseball has ever shone.

8

Peace

If 1945 had dropped a few hints that this might be a good time to get out of baseball, such as flinging me into a wheelchair and dropping A-bombs at the height of the season, 1946 obviously decided to quit playing games with me altogether: so 1946 went for my attention the old-fashioned way—it hit me with a rolled umbrella.

Not only did the English not play baseball, they gloried in not playing baseball. "Nothing but slogging, isn't it?" was the phrase, and they were not content to use it just once. "I mean, it's really just like rounders, isn't it?" That was the other phrase. "What's rounders?" "Oh *rounders*—ha ha ha. Well may you ask. Rounders *indeed*." Cough, splutter.

There's no need for you to suffer through the rest of this dialogue. Rounders was indeed a game where you ran around bases after hitting the ball, instead of charging straight at the pitcher's mound as in cricket. But why this made it a contemptible game, or even what was wrong with "slogging," I never quite made out. My English friends seemed to feel that they had said quite enough, and that their case against baseball was complete and airtight. And in all my years over there, I never heard a third sentence about baseball, except once when an old schoolteacher of mine from pre-war days, who used to bowl cricket balls at me between bouts of recurrent malaria, said out of nowhere, "You used to play baseball—you must be good at throwing." So somebody had noticed.

Fortunately, I was an old hand at talking to myself by now, and besides I had company, being perhaps the only boy in English public school history who has ever subscribed to *The Sporting News,* the baseball bible (which was actually a good thing to do—any eccentricity was better than none in that particular school). And it was in that journal, fading and ragged from its regular poundings by ships' luggage handlers and, by the looks of it, from being left out in the rain at Plymouth or Yarmouth or whatever, that I read how the Dodgers of '46 had lost a playoff to the Cardinals, with young Ralph Branca ominously losing the first game: no skin off my nose, or less than usual anyway, at that distance in space and time. The year was coming up for Christmas when word finally reached me.

But then, having waited so long, I was obliged to do my annual about-face in double-quick time, because the World Series began in the same issue, and I had to re-tool on the spot and start rooting for the Cards.

Never was this ungainly maneuver accomplished more gracefully or casually. In the cool of an English winter, with rugby players clattering all around and not another baseball fan for 3,000 miles, it is almost possible to take baseball calmly. And, on top of everything else, the Yankees weren't involved and I kind of liked the Red Sox. So I read the box scores like a rotisserie league fan before his time, hoping that Williams and Johnny Pesky and maybe Bobby Doerr (whose eyebrows reminded me of Rudolf Hess's but was otherwise okay) would get their hits but not quite enough to beat the Cards.

Obviously, St. Louis in seven was the perfect result, and Enos Slaughter scoring the winning run was more than perfect. It was a good year for the Dodgers to skip anyway. Next year I would catch up with them again somehow, after bribing the warden and sawing my way through the bars and hitching a ride across the Atlantic. At least, it was something to dream about as I removed the splinters from the oatmeal and defended the virtues of slogging to anyone who'd listen.

As it happened, getting back to America required no cunning at all—just a lot of whining. The long and short of it was that I came back to my favorite game as I'd come to it the first time, with fresh eyes and a slightly foreign mind. But first, in the early summer of 1947, the years or Fates had played their trump card, the only one that ever had a chance of working: they threw a beautiful woman into my cell to take my mind off my vows.

Dull minds may be startled to hear the stately old game of cricket described as a beautiful woman, but I can only say it looked good to me—and not just in the sense that the Martian girls begin to look good after a while. Cricket was in my blood anyway, in whatever curious way sports get into blood, and the way it was played in the English summer of 1947 would have knocked my eyes out in the middle of a pennant race. The sun shone practically every day, most especially at Lords cricket ground, my family seat (an ancestor of mine named William Ward once actually owned the place and played there too, an unusual double, and my cousin Wilfrid Ward is a life-member in consequence; if this perk had accrued to me instead of that good man, I probably would never have left England again and this story would be over just like that), where a wizard named Denis Compton seemed to be attempting, with the aid of some visiting South Africans who served as opponents, or straight men, to make England forget the war, or baseball or anything else that was on our minds. And I enjoyed every minute of it—only pausing occasionally to ask myself why on earth this was supposed to take my mind off baseball.

The batting was like baseball only more so, and the fielding was like baseball only less so, and the magic ingredient of base running had been simplified almost out of existence. But all this paled beside the fact that cricket was played with a bat and ball. And whatever their superficial differences, I found I could exchange the two sports at the airport as easily as one swaps pounds for dollars, and could pick up my place in the new baseball season and the flow of baseball history *almost* as if I'd never left.

Meanwhile my fling with cricket had illuminated something conceivably instructive about the nature of fan-ness— my fan-ness anyway: to wit, how much of it was and is in the head. As with baseball, my interest had first been baited by the printed word. My father had slyly given me a book on cricket the winter before we left the U.S. the way his Presbyterian relatives had once slipped him the notorious *Maria Monk* (a saga of sex in the convent) to lure him away from the Catholic Church.

I can only say that his book worked better than theirs. (If Jimmy Walker's famous phrase "No girl was ever ruined by a book" is really true, it only goes to show the difference between girls and boys: I have been ruined by more books than I can remember.) I'm not sure to this day *why* his book worked better, but maybe it was because Sir Pelham Warner's cricket book—I can't even remember its name—had pictures and the one he received didn't. I liked the motions of cricket on sight, with the bowler's arms windmilling in counterpoint to his legs, and the batsman flicking and slicing the results like a master chef, and I liked the patter underneath. "Victor Trumper's legendary cover drive. We shall not look upon his like again." Hey!

Phase I was complete. Phase II, actual exposure to the game in the murky summer of 1946, was something of a letdown. Where was "Prince Ranjitsinghi's leg glance" or "Sir Charles Fry demonstrates the late cut"? Come on guys. The game had gone to hell before I'd even gotten here. However, the summer wasn't a total washout. I learned the rules well enough to keep score for some school games, and I found that by faithfully copying the pictures in Sir Pelham Warner's book I could bat correctly enough in a nineteenth-century sort of way to draw the comment "Ah— you've had some coaching." Which, in the England of that day, probably also meant, you've been to a good school and come from a good family and can be counted on not to shoot your officers in the back.

Phase III was, as it had been with baseball, radio. The English team, or MCC, toured Australia in the winter of 1946–47, and much drama was added to its matches down there by the fact that we had to listen to them in the middle of the night, when everything that happens seems important. Now I was back safely in my head, dreaming of sunny skies and picture-perfect strokes in the midst of a grungy, godforsaken winter, and filling in the unearthly pauses (had the announcer had a stroke or what?) with palm trees and tropical groupies—an addition to every image that year. In that all-male dungeon of a school, I couldn't picture the House of Commons without groupies.

Once again a ball game, or the idea of a ball game, had come to my rescue. So when summer did finally break on England, I was off to Lords cricket ground to collect my prize and everyone else's for waiting through maybe the scruffiest, hungriest, longest winter in English history.

So the perfect game, the one they play in heaven, may be baseball or it may be cricket, but is without doubt a summer game wrapped in long cold winters and plenty of reading matter (before I'd even seen a good match, I could have done okay on a cricket trivia show). So we seemed to have a pattern here: and I've often wondered what life would be like in a bat- and ball-less society. Would one feel an itch in the missing limb? Would one reach blindly for a twig and a pebble and start swatting? And while you're stoking the fire, how about asking yourself how *Ted Williams* would have made out in such a world? Or Isaac Stern in a world without violins? Take your time about answering. Spring training is still three months away, and the MCC hasn't even reached Perth yet: they're still running pictures of deck games.

But now the 1947 baseball season is already ending. Well okay—it's a gift anyway, because I've already had the best part of a cricket season before my parents reluctantly return me to the United States, and there seems to be some juice left in this one too. Gionfriddo's catch for instance was still in there, and Floyd "Bill" Bevens's near no-hitter. In baseball, *any* game may be the one, and any moment may be the one too. After moseying along for seven innings of nothing much, you hear the announcer say "Gionfriddo seems to be drifting over"—and a second later something happens that you'll be looking at for the rest of your life.

So from that point of view, the best part of this season all lay ahead of me. And with this possibility always in mind I hopped on out to Ebbets Field the first chance I got, where the big news this year was Jackie Robinson, the first black anyone had ever seen in a big-league uniform, which seemed as strange to people then as a Chinese Coldstream Guard standing in front of Buckingham Palace. Jackie was modeling the uniform for literally scores of others, and he looked a little awkward at first base, but the awkwardness may have been mine.

Otherwise things had not changed too much around here, on the face of it. Leo Durocher was gone, of course, but I'd had since spring to get used to this since Leo's exile from baseball had been one of the rare sports events to make the overseas edition of *Time*. The same stable-cleaning impulse that had swept out booze after World War I turned its attention to the likes of Ingrid Bergman and Lippy this time around, and Leo was bounced for consorting with —George Raft and Laraine Day! The 1947 idea of bad companions stopped just this side of Dame May Whitty.

Of the players, Billy Herman had been traded to the Braves on grounds of old age (it never occurred to me that these guys were getting *old* in the service), and Cookie Lavagetto was trying to catch a little sun at the end of the dugout before shuffling off to St. Petersburg or wherever they sent ex-ballplayers to die (youth can be cruel). Mickey Owen had fled to the Mexican League as befitted a man living out his life on the run from disgrace, baseball's Lord Jim, and of course you need several games to take in which pitchers are missing. Durocher's own place had been taken by a road-company Connie Mack, Burt Shotton, whose demure street clothes protected him from any temptation to run out on the field or make trouble of any description. Uproar was dead.

Canceling these losses out with one swing of the bat was Reiser in center or left, depending, and Reese at short and Vaughan at third when he felt up to it. Dixie Walker was still here too, and wasn't that Hugh Casey out in the bull pen? Casey was sort of a Lord Jim himself on account of what happened *after* the third strike when he pitched like a condemned man and gave away what was left of the store—but some Lord Jims just don't get it and hang around anyway, and I was glad to see him.

As attrition goes, this wasn't too bad—on the face of it. What wasn't immediately apparent was that I had stumbled on the opening scene of *Beau Geste* where all the turrets are manned by corpses. Reiser had lost the divine spark as a hitter and fielder—though he still ran the bases and into fences like a scalded rat—Vaughan and Casey were on their last legs, and Walker was seething with unhappy confusion in right field over the Jackie Robinson question. Just a year before he had been "the People's Cherce," the most popular player in Brooklyn, and two years from now he would have been home free, as the *retired* "people's cherce" forever. But he had scotched all that in the spring by instigating an anti-Robinson petition and was now plunging straight for oblivion, by way of Pittsburgh whither Rickey was about to trade him.

What makes old Dixie a figure of mild pathos is that at the time, at least a few people probably said "Well—at least he sticks by his convictions." But within a single year these convictions would come to seem so fatuous that even he had begun to back away from them, defending Jackie publicly against Ben Chapman, the Phillie manager and redneck of the year, and even giving the "uppity" Negro some batting tips. But it was too late. If Dixie is remembered at all these days, it is as (1) a racist pig, (2) the guy they traded for Preacher Roe, or (3) Harry Walker's brother, any of which is quite a comedown from the People's Cherce.

So finally it all came down to Reese, who seemed to be better than ever, and the new guys, such as Carl Furillo in the outfield and Bruce Edwards, a brilliant catcher soon to be utterly eclipsed by, in close succession, a sore arm and Roy Campanella, and a kid throwing on the sidelines who *looked* more like a ballplayer than anyone I had ever seen. Duke Snider could have modeled for statues. This was it, the American ballplayer ready for the museums.

But as usual, the World Series came down to a bunch of names you had never even considered. Each year the newspapers run solemn comparisons of the teams, position by position, before the Series, but who bothers to scout the likes of Al Gionfriddo or Eddie Miksis, who scored the tying and winning runs in the Bevens game? Or, come to think of it, Floyd "Bill" Bevens himself? Or in other years all the guys named Martin or Hatcher who have lit the October sky like bonfires before returning to normal?

Nineteen forty-seven was the closest thing to a wacky World Series the prim, neat-freak Yankees ever found themselves in, although the one game I saw in the flesh looked like business as usual. This was game number 2 played at the Stadium, and it comes down in memory at least to a tale of two center fielders—Joe DiMaggio, who spent the afternoon catching line drives and canceling base hits just in back of second base, and Pete Reiser, the young god of 1941, who stumbled around the vast acres of Death Valley like an old man looking for his glasses. The trouble seemed to be something wrong with one of Pete's legs—though precisely what is still not certain, rumor running all the way to broken—and he sat out almost all the last five games, allowing him time for just one transcendent moment.

That 10–3 Yankee win remains the forgotten game of the
'47 Series—it really belonged in another one anyway. What
is remembered is the fourth game, which found me grimly
holding on to a bar stool at the Hotel Albert and marveling
at this new gizmo, television (I don't think this could have
been quite my first TV game, but it was close to it—so what
followed seemed all the more unreal on that pixilated day).

No game ever looked much less like a classic than this
one. Although it's true that the Dodgers couldn't buy a hit
off Floyd Bevens's fastball, this was at least partly because
they couldn't reach it. Ten walks is a long ways from a
perfect game, and it seemed possible at times that Bevens
and Yogi Berra, who was having a miserable maiden Series
behind the plate, might blow the whole game between
them without Brooklyn ever putting the ball in play.

As the game shambled along, with DiMaggio providing
one vintage over-the-shoulder catch and Rizzuto and Stanky
cementing one of baseball's purest and most beautiful
hatreds around second base, the bar began to fill up. It was
a weekday, and I had hoped to take in the whole game
before even the guys with the excuses began to get off work.
But this game was taking forever, and my seat at the bar was
beginning to look awfully good to the new arrivals.

"Will that be all, kid?" says the bartender. Everybody remembers games for different reasons, and I remember this
one best for the ginger ale I nursed through nine ugly,
eternal innings. I was sixteen, so it had to be ginger ale, and
I was broke, so it had to be one.

"Move it, kid," says the bartender. "In a minute," say I,
and make vague motions of departure, while the bartender
turns his back hopefully. It would violate the spirit of happy
hour to throw a crippled kid out in the street, and take up
valuable time as well, so he relied on killer bursts of moral
pressure. "You still here, kid? I thought I told you to move

it." "Yeah—in a minute, in a minute." "Look kid, I need the seat." "I haven't finished my drink." The customers look at him, look at me; I guess he's having a tough afternoon too. Meanwhile, another walk. And another. And a mound conference. What on earth is there left to talk about? "The plate is over there, so let's try to aim the ball in that direction—okay, Bill?"

But as Yogi was probably thinking at that very moment (and it ain't easy to catch and think at the same time, as he might say), "When it's finished it's usually over," and the game became a finished classic quite quickly and unexpectedly.

Gionfriddo walks, ho hum. Steals second, ho hum again. The Dodgers, who never run on anybody, steal seven on Berra in the Series, who will think and catch better in numerous future ones. Pete Reiser coming up to pinch-hit is better than ho hum, but only for a moment. They're going to, guess what, walk him—and that leaves exactly who to pinch-hit? Arky Vaughan has already *had* his walk for the day, so, oh Lord, out comes Father Time himself, old Cookie Lavagetto, still rusty from the service when he returned last year, but by now just rusty from rust and, unfortunately, right-handed to boot.

The best that could happen would be another walk, and maybe one more after that to send us into extra innings. On the plus side, though, I can't leave my seat now if I wanted to, but am jammed breastbone on wood against the bar by the latest wave of customers who are thrilled to find that there's still a game on and that they may even be in on the kill. If we imagine (I'm too proud to remember myself) that I might have had to go to the bathroom by this time, then my prayers for Lavagetto's success must have shaken heaven itself.

Of course, if I had known then what I know now, I too

could have waited till then to show up. The late arrivals missed nothing. On the other hand, if I'd had that knowledge I might also have known about Pete Reiser's leg, which would have heightened the moment even more as it still does when I watch the replay. Apparently Pistol Pete, using the one thing the war and various center-field walls had left him with, his guts, had dragged his battered limb all the way from the dugout to the plate without limping or betraying its true condition by so much as a blink—an astonishing feat, as I knew better than anyone—and had proceeded to take his four pitches like the Pete of old before tottering triumphantly down to first to be replaced by Eddie Miksis.

If the Yankees had known the kind of shape Reiser was really in, they could have pitched to him and defied him to run, and he would then have had to hit a home run like Kirk Gibson; and Reiser had hit only five all year. So we would have to call the intentional walk a Yankee mistake, would we not? Couldn't those klutzes do anything right?

The other thing the replay brings to mind is the terrible justice wrought upon Tommy Henrich in the next few minutes. In those early TV days, there was no way you could follow the ball off the bat, and since any roomful of people can always drown an announcer, the only way we could deduce that Lavagetto had even hit the ball into fair territory was to study the nearest fielder and try to figure out what he was up to. And in this case, the fielder was Henrich and what he was doing was scampering along the base of the trick wall in right like a cat chasing a ball of wool. The din in the bar and the nation's living rooms was amplified by the fact that we were coping with several layers of information at once and quizzing each other furiously about each of them. Had Bevins lost his no-hitter? ("Did he *have* a no-hitter?" asked somebody.) Had the Dodgers tied the game?

Had they conceivably *won* it? Had anyone ever seen anything like this?

The answer to all these questions depended squarely on
the public offender in right, so for a few precious moments
the whole of TV nation (a mere Liechtenstein compared
with today's version, but it seemed big at the time) trained
its gleaming eyes on the silent baggy-pants comedy of the
inimitable Tommy Henrich. Just six years before, in this
very park, this man had been the party of the first part to
Brooklyn's quintessential humiliation, the dropped third
strike, and it was clear from the way he manhandled Cookie
Lavagetto's game-winning drive off the right-field wall that
Henrich had been looking for ways to expiate the offense
ever since. I know, I know—he didn't field it *that* badly. But
to put it in a ballplayer's favorite tense: if Dixie Walker fields
that ball, only one run scores; if Furillo fields it, maybe *no*
runs score. Only a very guilty man plays it into two.

Then again, it *was* a tricky old wall, and maybe it wasn't
Henrich, maybe it was just the park itself getting even. What
may be harder to explain is the other irony of that creamy
rich day, which was that Hugh Casey himself wound up
credited with the win, after facing exactly one batter—
namely Tommy Henrich, who grounded as if mesmerized
into an inning-ending double play. Tell me this wasn't a
guilty man.

"The mills of God grind slow," as my father used to in-
tone when this kind of thing occurred in cricket, "but they
grind exceeding small." However, they never ground small
enough for the Yankees to lose a whole Series: like Red Sox
fans, we knew instinctively that we had to snatch our plea-
sures along the way from great fourth or sixth games.

The bar was bedlam—everybody turned out to be a
Dodger fan, or would be as soon as he was quite clear what

he'd just seen: the demented roars that had gone up had continued to defy the sound from the set and we pioneer TV watchers didn't really believe, or fully understand, the fuzzy pictures we'd seen until we'd *heard* from someone. In a moment I shall treasure forever, my enemy the bartender turned to me, all anger spent, and said, "What happened, kid?" Our contest was over too. Ten minutes from now, anyone could have the damn seat.

Meanwhile, uptown, a Yankee-minded friend of mine was taking appropriate steps to complete my happiness by flinging a glass coffee table against the living room wall in a blind fury. "It is not enough to succeed," as La Rochefoucauld says, "a friend must also fail." I've always preferred not to believe this about real life, but it's certainly true about sports, and not just on the field. That shattered table put the icing on the cake, a frustrated Yankee fan being in those days the kind of once-in-a-lifetime sight that bird-watchers kill for.

The next game was back to normal and so, after skipping a beat, was the seventh. If the second game was the forgotten one of the Series, it was not without strong competition from the other three Yankee victories. This was and is the price you pay for playing teams like the Red Sox and the old Dodgers. You will beat them of course, but the only games you will ever hear about afterwards and for the rest of your life are the ones in which *they* did something, for weal or woe. Even when old men gather around the fire to talk about the Mickey Owen unpleasantness the opposing Yankees just seem like onlookers at a tragedy. The real story is the Dodger stumbling toward his fate alone and falling on his sword by mistake.

In those terms, the only other game in the 1947 World Series was the sixth—"Gionfriddo's match," as the Brits would call it. But this one I saw with friends, so truth to tell,

I don't remember it that clearly. My lonely beachhead at the Hotel Albert bar had, it turned out, done my memory a service. The sheer desire for the game to end had screwed me to a pitch of concentration I have seldom attained at anything. But that kind of concentration would seem rude verging on bestial among friends, so you try to enjoy the game in a different way—a laid-back, jocular, South Seas sort of way. Ten years old forever. The Yankees are rallying, boo, the Dodgers are rallying, yea!, and "Hey Mahoney— you don't have to eat *all* the pretzels." In fact you're enjoying the Dodger rally a bit more than that, but you keep it within the convention of "my guys are better than your guys," and you won't remember a thing the next day.

All you finally have is the picture reinforced by a thousand replays, of Gionfriddo making the catch and DiMaggio kicking the dirt in response—if kicking isn't too strong a term for that gentle contemplative scuffing of the ground with the foot. DiMaggio's explosion of rage wouldn't have sent a ball of paper five feet. Clearly the man had lost all restraint in the war.

Strange to say this dreamy game, which fairly whizzes by in memory, actually lasted fifty-nine minutes longer than my ordeal of the other day, clocking in at three hours and nineteen minutes, the longest time ever consumed by a World Series game to that point. There were calls for reform the next day, led by a thirsty press whose workday had just been extended intolerably, and you can see for yourself how far these appeals have gotten us—3:19 would be considered quite normal these days, verging on the snappy.

The Yankees put us out of our misery the next day and, from a technical point of view, I guess it was an interesting game; at any rate, it was a breakthrough in anesthesiology. For the last five innings Joe Page blew smoke at the Dodgers, putting them to sleep one by one for the winter and shattering along the way all the canonical reasons for not using fastball pitchers in relief. The suspense, such as it was, came from waiting for Joe Page's arm to fall off. But, of course, it wouldn't. He was a Yankee and this was the World Series.

Last games tend to be elegiac anyway: the fans know that this is it for the season, there isn't going to be any more. Between now and the next ball games lurk rakes and tire chains and antifreeze. On top of which, the team that falls behind always seems to be fighting off narcolepsy with or without Joe Page's assistance, as if it knows what is coming, so why wait? According to the great military historian John Keegan, the "shock of battle" has usually dissipated sometime before the armies finally meet, and this tends to be true of seventh games, as it does of Wimbledon finals. The war has been decided earlier.

As if to emphasize the anticlimactic nature of seventh games, baseball regularly used to schedule them for Monday afternoons. So I along with millions of others neither saw nor heard the 1947 version, which was fine with me. With such games, the final score is quite enough information and quite enough commentary. And I appreciated the short sharp break with the season. "That didn't hurt, did it?" Yes it did. It hurt like hell. But the brisk air of a New York autumn would take care of it in no time.

9

In Which the Author Comes Perilously Close to Growing Up

Something changed after that.

Although I have followed other World Series just as closely as that one, and placed my nervous system on the same screaming roller-coaster, 1947 seemed like the last hurrah of the primal fan, the total obsessive who eats and sleeps baseball and won't let you into his cell if you don't say the magic word. I owed myself this one, after my sabbatical in England, and it could be that my enjoyment of that Series was as much an act of will as the gaiety at a class reunion; maybe I already knew I looked silly in that straw hat, but it was all part of the fun of being back in New York

—and I didn't mind if they caught me looking up at the tall buildings either.

But that was that. The minute the Series was over, or even a minute before, it was as if some celestial landlady had tapped me on the shoulder and said, "We're moving you and your friend to a smaller room now. You can take all your stuff up there and make almost as much noise, but we need the rest of the house." So, at least, it turned out. The baseball room in my head was a replica, a perfect miniature of the one I had had as a kid in the war, the good years, and when I went up there, I found I hadn't changed either: defeat was just as crushing, victory just as sweet and elusive, so long as I stayed in the room. But I didn't spend as much time there as before.

As I write this, the New York Mets have just lost four in a row and each game hurt for a second like the jab of a needle. That's something that doesn't get better or worse with the years. Pain is pain—an authentic link to childhood to be treasured. (Think of this the next time you see some old grad blubbering because the infants who represent his old school have lost a game: he may feel lousy, but that's the fountain of youth he's splashing around in.) But I had an antidote now of a kind they don't sell to children. I could always leave the room, and change the subject. You don't have to go abroad to forget about baseball.

A baseball fanatic doesn't arrive at this relative degree of sanity overnight, you can be sure. So long as the Dodgers stayed in Brooklyn, I spent a sinful amount of time in the baseball room, even though life and the exigencies of my green card kept jerking me around during most of those years and rubbing my nose in cricket (I inhaled deeply and kept going). By the time I settled in New York for good in August of 1955 the Dodgers were on the verge of leaving. So my view of those agony-ecstasy years is like a collage of snapshots taken in haste between arrivals and departures.

Thus, I was around for just enough of the '48 season to note that the Braves had the Aura about them around the batting cage, the Look, and were probably the team to beat this year (an observation not unique to me), before heading back to spend the rest of the summer watching the Australians play cricket. But then in '49 I reversed my steps and caught the *second* half or two-thirds of the baseball season, part of which I gobbled up on the first large TV I had seen, at the home of Henry and Clare Boothe Luce whom I've written about elsewhere, *not* a baseball household, so I had to keep it to myself as I had so many years ago—eight or nine years, half of a lifetime. That was a season when the Red Sox choked instead of us for a change (we just lost the regular way), but the image that sticks in my mind is of Stan Musial dominating the screen, as if they used a larger camera on him. Awesome.

And so it went, with a snatch of season here and a snatch there, with myself forever arriving breathless at Ebbets Field or one of the Bronx places, mightily relieved to find that nothing had changed, it was the same beautiful game, but mortally tired of seeing it with fresh eyes. Ebbets Field had come into its own, it was one of the few promises peacetime had kept, so that every day seemed like the feast day of some flamboyant saint, and I wanted to hang around awhile. Yet the constant highlighting that fresh eyes insist on stands me in good stead now as I remember those years; the excitement of watching new guys like Mantle and the incomparable Ernie Banks (Banks hit one so hard down the left line that I thought it was coming into the stands to get me), or old guys like Feller or the twitchy but stately Ted Williams, comes back all the clearer for being on borrowed time.

My Loony Tunes schedule, which would have driven a spy agency crazy if they'd been trying to figure it out—a cat going in and out the same door makes more sense—also whisked me a safe distance away from two extremely unpleasant episodes. The Bobby Thomson home run I have already mentioned, but I guess it won't quite kill me to look at it again. The Dodgers had already locked up the pennant to all intents and purposes when I headed back to England that August. Roger Kahn's famous Boys of Summer had hit their primes in a body just as the Cardinals were beginning to feel their ages. Branch Rickey was on *our* side now, and all was right with the world. It was like leaving a regiment of marines to guard the Bank of England for five minutes with no suspects in sight.

So safe did I feel that I scarcely bothered to glance at the U.S. baseball scores in the *Daily Express* which were printed without comment or elaboration on days when the paper got around to it at all, and buried invariably in gobbets of soccer trivia (Leeds United goalie says "I'm fed oop!") that only an anxiety case with a lot of time on his hands would bother to wade through. But on such days as I did catch the scores, the Dodgers seemed always to have lost and the Giants, of all people, to have won, and by mid-September this began to make me ever so slightly nervous. The *Express* might be a rotten paper with an anti-American bias—but why would they lie about a thing like this?

"It's just your imagination, go back to sleep." But I could swear I heard something and after a while the very austerity of the baseball news began to rattle me. *Say* something somebody! I assumed that even the *Express* would let me know when the Dodgers won the pennant, but they didn't, and pretty soon I began to claw at the paper and wade through "Everton forward says 'I've had enoof!' " as if life depended on it. But then I'd forget it again for the rest of

the day, because I wasn't *really* worried, was I? Nobody had
ever blown a 13-game lead, least of all this team and least
of all to the Giants. If it had been the Cardinals back there,
I'd be worried anyway, because the Cards had once put the
fear of God into me and left it there. But nobody feared the
Giants. They were the team old Irish drunks used to cry
over just before lights out, they were the past. If the Giants
had been a building, they would have been condemned
years ago. And all the Leo Durochers in the world couldn't
bring them back to life.

But Leo was the problem all right. Sinful old Leo had
been allowed back in the living room, but on the wrong
side of it, and I figured now that his style of kamikaze, live
for the moment, use the whole squad today and then use it
again tomorrow baseball might just conceivably buy you a
month or so of bliss before the crash. Bare scores, like a
bare stage, challenge you to write your own stories, and I
had goblins running up and down the aisles in mine before
this one was finished.

And then it happened: in the same expressionless tone as
if Anthony Eden were reading it, the *Express* said *First game
New York (N) 3 Brooklyn 1.* And even Lord Beaverbrook's
dastardly *Express* could not have invented a playoff. So the
impossible had happened. I had taken my eye off the upper-
case Bums for a few weeks and the lower-case bums had
gone and done it again. Against all odds, they had contrived
to blow another one. Almost ten years to the day after
"Mickey Owen's match."

By now the Dodgers' handsome comeback in the second
game of the playoff should not have fooled me (though it
did), because naturally they had to get up on their feet
before they could trip over them again and fall on their face
for the last time, in the ultimate bow, all the way into the
orchestra pit.

Not for one moment did I suppose that the Giants had had anything to do with it: we could handle this sort of thing perfectly well by ourselves. Meanwhile, in another part of the island, young George Plimpton was upending a bridge table at Cambridge University to express his more positive feelings about the outcome ("Rum chaps, Yanks"), and I believe that the *Express* may have broken its silence to mention a home run by R. Thomson, an ungovernable effusion by their standards.

It's possible that I may have told the cleaning lady about it too but I can't be sure because whatever quiet memory I might have had of that day has long since been drowned by crowd noises I've heard so often since and the demented cries of Russ Hodges: "The Giants win the pennant! The Giants win the pennant!" Ya de ya ya! Life had buffered me the best it could against this ghastly event, and in fact R. Thomson's home run didn't hurt that much at the time, as mortal blows go; but life could not spare me the replays. (Good National League soldier that I was, I grimly turned my guns around after that and aimed them feebly at the Yankees. But it didn't help. You didn't get miracles against the Yankees.)

The other misfortune that was softened by distance was one that had actually happened the year before, but I mention it second because it only began to hurt in combination with the Giant debacle: by itself it was kind of charming.

The Phillies' victory in 1950 on the last day of the season had reached me at Oxford around the same time as a surprise gift from a Nebraskan Fulbright scholar a few rooms away—namely the Sunday papers from his hometown of Lincoln, complete with a full set of funny papers, which can be the most reassuring sight in the world when you are trying to decide whether you have a serious case of homesickness or just the twenty-four-hour variety. (For all my travels, my homesicknesses all ran in the same direction, to where the ballparks were.)

So the two are inextricably linked in my mind: the funnies and the Phillies, a marriage made in Disneyland. The Philadelphia victory that year was exactly the kind of thing that might have happened to Joe Palooka himself. Or possibly to Dagwood Bumstead in his dreams ("Wake up and walk the dog, honey"). Their very name, "the Whiz Kids," sounded like an unsuccessful comic strip. Although I had never given my heart to the Phillies—one ridiculous romance was enough per city, and the A's at least had a past —only a low-life cat-kicker, or an ugly sister, could have begrudged them their solitary trip to the altar in 1950, or their respectable showing (three pitching duels and a blowout) against the Yanks—who were on the brink of the Mantle era and could have been taken. I was only sorry it had to be at the expense of the Dodgers.

Sorry? In the light of 1951, I was apoplectic. Was there no team, so lowly and undistinguished, so lame and halt, that it *couldn't* walk over the Dodgers at the last minute? Who had appointed us nature's doormats, anyway? Once upon a time, I'd read an article in *Baseball* magazine entitled "Is There Sentiment in Baseball?" which concluded, as I recall, that there was no room for the stuff but that it got in anyway. I would try to remember the first part of this proposition the next time some club came sniveling to the door in rags saying "Please sir—we haven't won a pennant in thirty-five years. Would the Dodgers let us have one of theirs?" Baseball is full of hard-luck cases, Clevelands and Chicagos, but, as I would soon be learning from the old Boston Bees (now Braves, and soon not Boston either), give them an inch and they'll take a dynasty.

Obviously, I'd missed a step on my travels if I took these opponents of ours so lightly. It was no disgrace to lose a pennant to Robin Roberts and Curt Simmons, I actually knew that because I'd seen them, but Larry Jansen and Sal Maglie sounded like the kinds of names that teams brought up in September, never to be heard from again. Had we really lost to *them?* Or had the entire Dodger team died in a plane crash or been sent to Korea? Even a minimalist needs *something* to go on, but in my travels I had shaken off *The Sporting News*—which I picture still circling the globe slowly in various tubs looking for me in Fiji or Borneo. And even a team-specific outbreak of the Black Death would not have cracked the *Daily Express.*

Feeding on scraps, an occasional item in *Time* or the *Paris Tribune,* I got through the season of 1952 somehow without touching down in the United States at all. This was living dangerously, and '52 was probably the year I came closest to the dreaded condition of being able to take baseball or leave it alone. Maybe it would all just slip away one day. I'd reach back and come up with a fistful of indifference. I'd seen it happen. Frisky little baseball fans who wore suits now and looked at you queerly if you brought the subject up, as if you'd just whipped a baby's rattle out of your pocket.

Yet as I look at the record books, and at Roger Kahn's marvelous book, 1952 seems as familiar as any other year and I feel as if I must have been here all along. Such is the sweep of baseball history that it picks up for you in your absence and fills you in upon your return like a chatty landlady (landperson?) who is always bursting with news for you. And I could swear I saw with my own eyes Billy Loes losing the ground ball in the sun—Dodger highlights are not like other people's—as the Bums found yet another, absolutely unique way to lose to the Yankees.

Well, at least we were losing to a better class of people again. And for the rest of these gorgeous twilight years while the Dodgers remained in Brooklyn, there would be no more disgraces, only regular heartbreaks, and a lot of glory.

Nineteen fifty-three was a great year to be back, and I waved the most perfunctory of kisses at the soil before heading off to Ebbets where the party was in full session— and what a party it was. One hundred five victories, count 'em, and career years for everyone! Furillo, Hodges, Campy, the Duke, and the incomparable Jackie, breaking out of rundowns like Captain Marvel and setting infielders to gibbering—every one of these titans at his laughing best (except Furillo, who glared). Of them all, the one I see first and most clearly as I write this is Roy Campanella, built fat and comfortable to put you in a good mood but with the most stern and perpendicular of bats and a stroke like a whip. And you might as well try to slide around a sofa when he was blocking the plate.

The trick the Dodgers had contrived for losing to the Yankees that year was, I decided, possibly the only one that would have worked: Don Newcombe got drafted, leaving us a pitcher short. All in all, the Korean draft didn't amount to much by World War II standards; it was barely a blip on the screen of baseball history. But such as it was, this sad excuse for a draft clearly wanted its few depradations to be noticed, so it took Ted Williams and it took Newk. (Okay, and it took Willie Mays. So what?)

It was during that fall that I began to form a theory, which after thirty-some years of mulling and whittling I passed on to George Will, who in turn passed it on to Ralph Kiner and Tim McCarver in the broadcasting booth of the Mets, where it sits to this day—to wit, that the teams that break your heart are the ones that play in funny stadiums, and always for the same good reason. Their pitching staffs are shot by autumn. Try pitching in Fenway Park or Wrigley Field or

Ebbets Field, if you can find it and put it together again, for a whole summer and you'll see what I mean. Your arm is ragged from hitting spots and your nerves are gone from paying for every mistake—and occasionally paying for good pitches too. And in breeze the Yankees.

Contrariwise the old Yankee Stadium with its distances intact must have been a swell place for a pitcher to spend the summer, especially with DiMaggio or Mantle in back of him. Mickey's fielding tends to be forgotten, because his arm went back on him halfway through his career after he stepped in a pothole—well, it's a long story—and because his fielding style was so understated. I remember once looking at the three Yankee outfielders and trying to guess which of these three motionless men the ball had been hit to (you had to find *something* to amuse yourself with, after the score reached 10–0). At the last second, the Mick raised his hand, and that was that.

The 1953 Series hurt. I hadn't had my heart broken from up close for several years, but this time there was no *Daily Express* and no funny papers from Nebraska to act as a scrim between me and reality—nothing but a black-and-white screen which I studied intensely for signs of choking. Surely a team that faints at the sight of a finishing line must have some deep character flaw, but I couldn't find it then and I can't find it now in the record book. The fielding could have been tighter, but the guys who made the errors— Hodges and Furillo and Campanella—were the least likely suspects and had fielded just fine in other Series as well as batting splendidly in this one—a collective .300 average is almost unheard of against anybody, let alone against Reynolds, Raschi, Lopat, and a young Whitey Ford, and is enough to take the hitters off the hook in perpetuity, both for this choke-season and for all the others they played in. So it really had to be the pitching, which didn't so much choke that year as splutter to a halt. *I don't care how close we are, boss, I can't pitch no more.* (Pitchers seldom choke, they're too busy. And when they appear to, I'm reminded of Arnold Palmer's dictum about golf: "Non-players have no idea how many things can go wrong with your game besides choking.")

And so, steaming helplessly by the side of the road, we leave the 1953 Dodgers. By this time, I'd heard of the Giants all right, and was properly apprehensive about the return of Willie Mays and the acquisition of Johnny Antonelli—a fireballer who hadn't quite found himself—from the Braves, but I missed their heroics in 1954 by the unusual expedient of being in Australia, visiting the family seat. It was there, about as buffered as a man could be, that I saw a newsreel film of Willie Mays making his famous catch off Vic Wertz and heard the short overseas version of how a layabout named Dusty Rhodes had made nonsense of the form book, before returning to his park bench to sleep.

Well, good for them. But it *was* only the Indians and you couldn't really call yourself world champions until you'd beaten the Yankees. On the whole, I was more interested in the movie that came with the newsreel, *Les Enfants du Paradis,* I think it was.

(That was some catch, though. History records a similar one that Joe DiMaggio made off Hank Lieber in the '36 Series, which ended with Joe cantering straight into the center-field clubhouse. But in those days legend had to do duty for tape, so Willie's catch remains *the* World Series catch, and the best image we will ever have of what baseball might be like if they took away the fences altogether.)

If this were a cricket book, the winter of 1954–55 would actually deserve one of the longer chapters, but as it's not, I'll just add that I saw a lot of great tennis too (Seixas and Trabert *v.* Rosewall and Hoad), and experienced a dream come true to the point of tedium: one afternoon in the Adelaide Pavilion, I met so many of the athletes representing England and Australia at cricket that I couldn't remember why I'd ever wanted to. Not that they weren't nice fellows—but what was the point? It was like visiting Hershey, Pennsylvania, and eating chocolate all day.

The one thing I did learn from it, and subsequent meetings with athletes seem to bear it out, is that the stars, with dazzling exceptions, are the dullest, while the best talkers tend to be bit players, relief pitchers or other professional substitutes who are living on their wits. *That* one might have guessed. But otherwise, a room full of athletes can be like the most average pub you've ever been in anywhere.

Australian cricket peters out in February and the tennis players head north on their endless rounds and it's none too soon to start cadging bits of baseball news, of which the Australian general press carries a little, and *Time* and *Life,* when you can find them, carry a little bit more, and it doesn't take much of this to start the engine purring. As the half-baked Australian winter goes into its number, huffing and puffing like a real winter, the Dodgers come bursting out of the starting gate with blood in their eye. Ten in a row, drop a stitch, eleven in a row. This is the year, and no excuses.

I am due back in August, but I don't care if the race is all over by then. After a deprived childhood, I don't need even the mild discomfort of suspense, but, if you change the name of the team, I subscribe wholeheartedly to Colonel Jake Ruppert's definition of a perfect game, which was for the Yankees "to score nine runs in the first inning and then *slowly* pull away."

The only trouble with such a game, or season, is that it

doesn't leave you a hell of a lot to talk about, or write about. The Dodgers seemed to be practically taking curtain calls when I arrived, which meant that for once they might enter the World Series as well rested as the Yankees, who usually seemed to clinch their pennants around Labor Day (although even when some pretender made a race of it with them, they *still* seemed rested).

The only real news that August was the first faint but unmistakable death rattle of the Brooklyn Dodgers. Baseball fans are used to this sort of thing by now. Just when things are going indubitably well, your star player announces that he's desolately unhappy here and probably won't be back next year. Okay—no big deal. Bobo is just testing the waters. Whenever there is no hard baseball news, there will be soft, which means stuff like this. Next February, Bobo will be singing a different tune and you'll have to listen to that too, about how your city contains the best fans in the world, and the best schools and parks and inland waterways, and about how he wants, his accountant willing, to end his career nowhere but here. It will no doubt make you feel kind of proud to live in the same town and share the same space as Bobo.

But baseball had not yet taken off like a hot air balloon in 1955, and we weren't used to O'Malley's brand of flightiness. Although the Brownies had lit out for Baltimore two years earlier, and the A's for Kansas City, and the Bees now definitely Braves to Milwaukee, these teams had been officially dead for a long time now, even the Braves, whose 1948 pennant may rank as baseball's most unusual out-of-body experience, and in each case their fans had largely gone over to the other team in town. All the other major-league teams were respectably tethered to their cities, and the ballplayers were tethered to their teams, and a man could enjoy a pennant race in peace.

So, on top of his other sins, O'Malley sent a chill through our finest hour. Businesswise it was probably a great time to do it. The Dodgers were never going to be more popular than right now; as it happened, this particular team was just beginning to turn, and it might take years to build another one, since almost all the parts would have to be replaced at the same time. If Rickey had stayed, he would already have traded half of them and tapped the farm system for the likes of Roberto Clemente. But Rickey had long since been eased out by the brutish O'Malley, and he had recently kidnapped Clemente himself to Pittsburgh as a form of revenge. It was hard to hate *anyone* that year, but O'Malley was testing us.

Apart from anything else, the form of his latest threat was so demeaning: he was going to start phasing Dodger games into Jersey City! (It's the nature of metropolitan neighbors to despise each other and I'm sure Jersey fans would feel just as demeaned if their teams were sent to Brooklyn.) So. Joisey City? This guy must be kidding, no? But O'Malley did not look like a kidder.

All right—we'll worry about that when we come to it. Some real and welcome hard news was looming in the form of the Yankees and 1953 had taught me, as if I didn't know it already, that no Dodger team was so good on paper, or Yankee team so vulnerable on the same substance, that the rascals couldn't sneak past us at the last minute. Just because the Yanks had lost Raschi, Reynolds, and Lopat and you'd barely heard of the new guys didn't mean that they didn't still have better pitching than we did.

And indeed, paper flew out the window as the Dodger pitching stars this time turned out to be Johnny Podres and Roger Craig, whoever they were—the kind of semi-knowns you expected the Yankees to beat *you* with—while Don Newcombe, my excuse for 1953, wound up with an E.R.A. of 9.53. Nineteen fifty-five even boasted its very own Al

Gionfriddo—an ethnic miracle-man in left field named Sandy Amoros, who did to Yogi roughly what Al had done to DiMag. (History does not record whether Yogi kicked the dirt, because all the cameras were trained on first base where Gil Hodges was waiting for Amoros's throw to come panting in to double off Gil McDougald. *Everything* was better in 1955.)

A Dodger fan finds himself tongue-tied in the presence of success, but this one was every bit as sweet as it was supposed to be—all the more so because it came after two defeats, a rocking left and a right from Whitey Ford and Tommy Byrne, respectively. Our own wrecking crew took over in the three middle games at Ebbets Field in what turned out to be the penultimate hurrah of the Boys of Summer, with Duke Snider presiding: three homers spread over games 4 and 5.

Game 6 at the Stadium was the throwaway game this time, the one nobody remembers, and by chance it was once again the one I attended in person. It didn't seem throwaway at the time but heavy with bad omens, like a premature seventh game, with the lights already beginning to flicker. The Dodgers had had their fun at home, but facing Whitey Ford at Yankee Stadium was like waking up in the bin at Bellevue Hospital. The revelry was over now and the cowbells and the sym-phonies that had seemed such fun at the party last night were nothing but a dim, throbbing memory. And here was Doctor Ford to tell us the facts of life.

That sixth game was a quiet one even by midweek Philadelphia standards, so by Brooklyn standards it was like dawn in an Ingmar Bergman movie. Nobody ever brought a cowbell or a trombone to Yankee Stadium, although I expect Death showed up there on his afternoons off. Such as this one.

So this is where it all went wrong every year, this is where

it died. The past did not so much flash before my eyes as
crawl past banging funeral drums. Never mind what you'd
done in April, or even September. It was all the same to the
Yankees. Once you entered this house, you had no past.
You were in the palace of the Grand Inquisitor now, where
all infidels were treated alike, and even the visiting Dodger
fans booed in whispers.

On the more technical side of things, the Dodgers
seemed further handicapped by the prevailing superstition
that you would die a spinster if you tried to hit the ball to
the opposite field: real men pulled the ball, and the Brooklyn righties spent the balance of the afternoon either whal-
ing Whitey Ford's low-breaking stuff straight at the third
baseman and shortstop, or striking out in the attempt. The
fruit of their All-Star exertions came in the end to precisely
four singles, two of them to left, and three outfield flies—
one of them to left. No wonder Ford (who was a kind of
left-handed Orel Hershiser and must have loved the low
National League strike zone) had such a great World Series
record in his prime.

Meanwhile, Moose Skowron, who had no such supersti-
tions, was hitting a three-run homer almost into my lap in
the lower right-field deck as a species of calling card, like
an arrow flying through your window in a Western. This is
how you do it, gentlemen. And on top of that Duke Snider,
our last best hope for the seventh game in Yankee Stadium,
sprained his wrist. Hemlocksville. I had read somewhere
that our very own batting champ Carl Furillo had described
batting slumps as beginning with (a) a game where you hit
the ball hard but unsuccessfully followed immediately by
(b) a game where you go 0 for 4 against a breaking-ball
pitcher. And even though we had skipped (a), we had certainly just come down with a raging case of (b), with Tommy
Byrne, who'd already given us a whipping in game 2, on tap

to rub it in the next day, and only this guy Podres left to pitch for us. And we didn't even know yct, because Yogi hadn't worked it out yet, that "it ain't over till it's over."

So I, along with several million others, was beautifully primed and conditioned for an unexpected triumph the next day: we had raced through our own hurry-up Lent, and glanced into the abyss—it didn't take long, because we'd seen it before—and were perched on our bar stools waiting for another typical seventh game, with autumn beginning to move in sometime around the fifth or sixth inning, and the ground crew peeping like rats out of the shadows, eager to get it over with, and the fans, who'd paid a king's ransom for seats, drifting away from baseball for the year before it died in front of their eyes.

And you know the rest. The Dodger batting slump indeed came to pass, and Duke Snider, no doubt favoring his wrist, was not much help, striking out twice and grounding out to second. We got all in all five hits and the Yankees got eight. And that's absolutely all the bad news I can think of from that day of days.

The game observed final-day traditions by being a minimalist Stadium affair, with the Amoros play standing out like a scream; and as the ninth inning wound down, it turned out that Gil Hodges, that most satisfying of New York heroes, had driven in the only two runs of the game. So it was only fitting that Pee Wee Reese should toss him the winning ball at the end of the game. The fact that the ball was still in play, and that Reese's throw was a wee bit off line, only added to the unholy glee that exploded in a million bars and living rooms and offices and came pouring into the streets of Brooklyn on a wave of pure happiness. Even in Manhattan, true believers pounded each other's backs and howled as if we were off some place in the woods instead of clustered tight around that office radio, or wherever we were. (I myself watched ceremonially at the bar of the Hotel Albert, where I no longer had to nurse a single ginger ale. Scotch and water is the best revenge.)

"I did not love as others do/none ever did, that I heard tell on." My father's words come back to me again as I remember Gil Hodges's mitt closing on the ball like the door of a bank vault: throwing it to him was indeed like depositing it in the Bank of England, and no monkey business this time. Certainly no celebration *I've* ever taken part in has been quite like that one. Even the noise, which is usually just noise at such times, indistinguishable from one event to another, sounded more amiable than usual, but that may just have been my fancy. What was unique about this one was the quiet satisfaction of it, and sense of vindication. Wherever we had spent the intervening years, part of us had been waiting with an ear out for this to happen. And now that it had, one imagined cheers going up in jungle clearings, and organ lofts and opium dens, and wherever Dodger fans were to be found. We felt collectively like Hercules after his twelve labors: now at least we could put up our feet and turn off the phone. Victory has, as noted, a way of letting you down, of not tasting quite as good as it looked on the menu. But not this one—this one tastes sweet even today, despite the bitter aftertaste that comes a second later.

If Walter O'Malley had deprived us of this too, I doubt he would have left town alive.

10

After Many a Summer Dies the Dodger Fan

O'Malley hadn't been kidding about New Jersey. The Dodgers opened in Roosevelt Stadium, Jersey City, before 12,000 or so baseball-starved fans—a number Brooklyn could have topped any Monday, in February, in a blizzard. Obviously, after the novelty wore off, Jersey was going to be some kind of promised land all right—the kind of bonanza that George Steinbrenner would no doubt have blamed on his marketing people.

So what, outside of hurting our feelings, did O'Malley suppose he was doing this time? The politicians he was trying to frighten into handing him a new stadium complete with half the borough to park in budged maybe half an inch or so, by setting up a board to do something or other. But you couldn't seriously threaten anyone with Jersey City, the ultimate empty gun. The thing is, I had *been* to Roosevelt Stadium when it was owned by the Giants, and even if it had been new and improved (which it wasn't), the place was minor league down to its girders. And the Hague machine or whatever was running Jersey City at the time certainly wasn't about to replace it with the kind of pleasure palace O'Malley seemed to have in mind. The Fat Man was obviously just trying to build a case against the New York pols, who God knows made it as easy as they could for him, as the real culprits who spinelessly let the Dodgers get away from Brooklyn, rather the way Harry Truman *lost* China for the West. But to this day, his case has not been made, for reasons I'll suggest in a moment, and it certainly wasn't helped by his embarrassing, mind-boggling little Jersey ploy.

At any rate, it did start the bad blood flowing and it was helped along in a small way by a daffy little article by Duke Snider that summer entitled "I Play Baseball for Money Not Fun," which might have been ghostwritten by Walter O'Malley himself. In Snider's book, *The Duke of Flatbush,* the author says that some neutral remarks of his about the big-league life had been heightened slightly and teased into a whine, and since we're not talking about the 1919 World Series or anything momentous, his word should be good enough for anyone by now. But I remember the episode quite well because it occasioned the only atmosphere of ambiguity I've ever encountered in a ballpark. We didn't really want to boo the Duke—but we *were* sort of mad at him, weren't we? The night I went, the culprit himself seemed to slink out to center field as if he wished there were some way of arriving there in an unmarked envelope.

Ebbets Field seemed for a moment to pulse with embarrassment like an English living room.

But only for a moment. We loved the Duke for reasons that had nothing to do with his writing, and even in his writing, he now swears that he loved Brooklyn too—his account of his old neighborhood has the *details* of a real love affair—and Dodger fans were too effervescent and intelligent to hold grudges against our own players. (Case in point: when Gil Hodges went 0 for 21 in a World Series, the borough *prayed* for him, for pitysake; in Shea Stadium they would have tried to lynch him. But Gil Hodges had a great Series the next year, whereas Darryl Strawberry went to Los Angeles. And that's what I mean by intelligent.)

The fans were also far from jaded after their victory last year. It would take a lot more than one world championship to do that (twenty seems like a good number for how many we needed). So far, we had only proved that it *could* be done. Now we had to move in for the kill, which, as I saw it, would be no ordinary pearl-handled, la-di-da self-defense affair but a ritual gangland payoff, with the boys pumping lead into the Yankees like there's no tomorrow. "We're sending a message to your boss." I myself had finally settled down in New York and was looking forward to a feast of gore over the next few years uninterrupted by ocean voyages or last-minute departures.

Ah, the dreams of winter. Actually in the cool gray light of history, one sees why O'Malley was nervous. Judging from their ages and the rings around their bark, it looks now as if the current gang was quite lucky to fire off a single last round before retiring to the farm. Jackie Robinson, the soul, or animating principle, of the team, had just about had it and was down to spot duty. Reese at thirty-eight was mighty old for a shortstop. And everybody was a touch more crotchety, causing Snider to loosen up his tonsils once again, this time to blast his fellow teammates for criticizing manager Walter Alston anonymously in the press.

As far as I could see, using anonymity against Alston was only fighting fire with fire. Following on the heels of the two most colorful managers in baseball, Chuck Dressen and Leo Durocher, Alston seemed like a complete cipher even after his championship last year, a fifties caricature who wore his uniform like a gray flannel suit in search of a briefcase, and if the players didn't like him either, what precisely was keeping him here?

But turning on the history light again, one sees that the amiable Alston was more of a portent than we realized. After the triumphant season of 1953, Chuck Dressen had very reasonably asked for a two-year contract and been turned down, because the Dodgers (O'Malley always called himself "the Dodgers") did not believe in two-year contracts. This was news to us, but it wasn't too hard to understand how a man might get tired of Chuck Dressen: Chuck was the kind of chirpy, boastful, cock sparrow of a man who isn't quite charming enough to be allowed center stage for long and can perch on your nerves and jangle them if you have to read about him every day, for all his incomparable skill at stealing other teams' signs.

So we sat back confidently wondering which of the good old boys from the managers bar and grill would be tapped to entertain us next. Someone like Jimmy Dykes or Birdie Tebbetts would be just fine—a raconteur who could get off a good line occasionally. Personality was everything in Brooklyn and auditions really should have been held in the back of a taxi. Frankie Frisch would be kind of boring. "Oh, those bases on balls" is not that great a line. But acceptable. Casey Stengel was too much to hope for.

But "the Dodgers" walked right past the boys in the back

room and headed for the nearest milk bar. The choice of Alston was not quite unprecedented (Joe McCarthy never played in the big leagues either) but it was close enough, and it carried almost more symbolism than a strictly baseball move should be asked to bear. O'Malley was, in effect, thumbing his nose at the whole Dodger tradition. He didn't, he was telling us in everything but words, *like* good old boys and he didn't like color. In fact, he probably didn't even like Brooklyn, which is full of both, or tradition itself, with its insistence on continuity.

O'Malley's taste for one-year contracts suggests that no manager would ever become a fixture here again, in the style of Durocher or the great Wilbert Robinson—that's to say a Brooklyn personage in his own right with his own popular base of support that might rise up in wrath and raspberries if you fired him. Future managers would be chained tightly to the front office, like the pens they use in banks, and would be answerable only to him. They would also at all times, even after a good year, keep their bags packed and their eyes trained over their shoulder where they would see nothing but O'Malley, the Buddha as bank manager, the ultimate Frank Capra villain.

Perhaps, who knows?, he even wanted a manager who would feel at home in the bland air of Southern California. Human cash registers like O'Malley aren't always the best judges of people, so he might have been mildly surprised by the way in which the borough finally took to Alston, after Snider had cleared the air (*we'll* provide the color, for Alston as we had for Dixie Walker, you just be yourself), or contrariwise, the way Los Angeles would someday embrace Tommy Lasorda, a movie version of a colorful, Brooklyn-type manager.

Since 1956 was my first full baseball season since the war, I found myself looking into its pores more closely than usual and noticing clubhouse glitches like the Snider ruckus the way the daily press has to, with a possible blur-ring of the big picture. If one steps back again a thousand miles or so, one sees a great team on its last legs, with Snider and Hodges covering the retreat with their bats and Newcombe taking care of the pitching in a last herculean effort, along with the ultimate samurai, an unshaven wet-back from across the Bronx River, Sal Maglie himself. As Freddy Fitzsimmons had once crossed this same river to give the Dodgers the 1941 pennant, and Durocher had later crossed back to help the Giants settle scores in 1951, now along came Maglie, like a right-handed pitcher to be named later, to complete the deal.

There is no friend like an ancient enemy, and Brooklyn had no serious trouble accepting Sal the Barber after the first round of boos—although Maglie's opening conversa-tions with Furillo and Robinson must have taxed their re-serves of politeness and had them reaching for their Amy Vanderbilts. Otherwise, you had to like a guy who looked like Willard Mullin's epic portrait of the Brooklyn Bum—especially when he wins 13 games for you and pitches his mean little heart out against the universal enemy in the World Series. Sal should have been with us all along, and by the end of the year we felt as if he had.

But it was ominous that the old gang had to send outside for help from anyone, and once again, a dispassionate ob-server—of which there were none in Brooklyn, except by chance the icy O'Malley—would have noted that the Milwaukee Braves with Aaron and Mathews and Spahn were the coming team and the Dodgers were the going team, and that if he, Walter, hoped to blackmail the city, or any other city, into financing his dreams, he'd better keep moving on it.

Luck, I suppose, was on O'Malley's side, because the Dodgers pushed their way past the Braves at the last minute like senior citizens demanding their rights, and would go on to provide one of their most beguiling defeats, a classic to go with their collection—not so much a swan song as a goose song, as befitted their role in folklore. It took a very fine team to get as far as they did every year but it took the Dodgers to run into the only perfect game ever pitched in a World Series. And perhaps it would have been wrong to leave town on any other note: otherwise, how would one have known it was the Dodgers? Anyone can *win*.

Once again, the rest of the 1956 World Series recedes in the presence of the one super-catastrophe. But up to that point, it had been a cheerful little Series. The Dodgers, now that they knew how easy it was, had annihilated the opposition in the first two games at Ebbets Field, and only needed to take one of the three at the Stadium to annihilate them again in game 6. But the Yankees had come to life in their home mausoleum and now, two games later, we still needed that one win and had, truth to tell, begun to sweat ever so slightly. It might prove difficult to annihilate the bums twice at home.

On the plus side, though, the Yankees were down to using Don Larsen, a scatter-armed roustabout we'd already dispatched once in game 2, and our guys were still loose from last year and the prospect of home cooking this year. For once, the ancient law of subway Series which decrees that there shalt be no day of rest in between games had worked in our favor instead of shredding us; because this year, *we* had the ace in the hole, in the shape of Sal Maglie, and they didn't.

Of the unique disaster that followed, there is possibly only one thing to be said that hasn't been said a hundred times already, and that is that Babe Pinelli was working behind the plate that day, and Pinelli had a rather eccentric view of balls and strikes. As he would later make clear in an article printed in Charles Einstein's epic *Fireside Book of Baseball,* Pinelli belonged to the A-for-effort, or Little League, school of umpire which maintains that so long as the pitcher comes *close* to the corners of the plate, he has tried and should be rewarded with a strike.

To make matters worse, Pinelli was umpiring his last big-league Series, so we can assume his eyes were bleary with tears—at least when he called the final strike of the game against Dale Mitchell, a contact hitter who had never struck out *once* in twenty-eight previous World Series at-bats and had seldom taken a called third strike in any kind of game.

More remarkably yet, Don Larsen, who had walked four guys in the one and a half innings he'd worked last time, only went as high as three balls on a single hitter on this day of days.

So are we talking about a game that will live in infamy or what? It was as if Babe Pinelli had forgotten who was supposed to get the gold watch today. And so Sal Maglie's gutsy five-hitter was wasted, along with Gil Hodges's prodigious line drive in the fifth which Mantle flagged down with one of the great World Series catches of all time.

Although it wasn't part of Carl Furillo's prescription for slumps, every batter knows that losing your confidence in the strike zone is like losing your compass in the woods, and the Dodgers could barely buy a run after that even in Ebbets Field which practically handed runs to you on the way in. The only one they did score for the remainder of the Series was a classic case of "What goes around comes around" which can strike at any time and has no connection with normal probabilities.

No one had done more to make Jackie Robinson's first year in the big leagues unrelievedly miserable than Enos "Country" Slaughter of North Carolina, who had attempted to cut off Jackie's ankles, between curses, the very first time they met. So there he stood now in left field exactly ten years later, with two outs in the bottom of the tenth and runners on first and second and Robinson at bat. And what should happen but that Robinson hits a line drive straight at him—the dirtiest trick you can play in baseball—and Slaughter comes in on it like a rookie, only to watch it sail derisively over his head to bring in the winning run. Short and sweet, a simple message from me to you. Baseball grinds on, producing hundreds of games between this event and that, and I doubt if a single other person in the park remembered the shared history of these two guys, the hero and the goat of game 6. "It was just personal," as Gatsby would say.

And that was it. Clem Labine, who, along with Carl Erskine, constituted the very heart of the Brooklyn pitching staff, had shot the Dodgers' last bolt with his ten-inning, seven-hit masterpiece. It would be Labine's role this year as it had been in the play-off of 1951, and hence in history, to be the last Bum to shake his fist at the enemy before the roof fell in. (A Dodger commemorative stamp would have to reflect either this, or Jackie Robinson stealing home, or conceivably Duke Snider drawing an intentional walk so "they" could get at the righties. Or, or.)

The seventh and last Series game ever at Ebbets Field was a quintessential last game anywhere with all the suspense and giddy laughter of a Japanese No play. The Yankees put us away early and they put us away often. They pounded on

Don Newcombe—casually destroying for all time my excuse for losing in '52 and '53—and then they pounded on Roger Craig, who is currently the philosopher in residence at Candlestick Park. And when the time had come for Erskine to close the joint ceremonially in the ninth, the Yankees were ahead 9–0, which is the exact score the rules dictate for a forfeit game in which one of the teams doesn't show up at all. The last World Series home run in Ebbets Field was a grand slam by Yogi Berra, and the last Dodger putout went from Reese to Hodges, as it had last year, the old two-man holding company in good times and bad.

Afterwards Roger Craig could at least have said that he needed the experience. Six years from now, he would star as the losingest pitcher on the losingest team in history, the original New York Mets, so it didn't hurt him to have a Dodger World Series under his belt. But Newcombe didn't have even a facetious consolation that day. Although his very first game against the Yankees had been a thrilling 1–0 defeat in the 1949 Series (Henrich's winning home run is about all anyone can remember of that whole Series), this performance did not, as it should have, dispose of the charge that he always "choked" against the Yanks.

To be sure, the Bombers had gotten his number after that, as they had so many people's numbers—it was no disgrace to be in the Yankees' black book—but only an amateur could suppose that professional baseball games are determined primarily by the contestants' nervousness. Fans caught in the act of making life miserable for hometown heroes should be made to write out a hundred times the quote of Arnold Palmer's cited earlier *vis-à-vis* the number of things that can go wrong with your game besides choking. And Arnie was just talking about golf, a game you play by yourself: imagine trying to play it against the New York Yankees.

However, the stands tend to be full of amateurs, and most of them that day must have supposed that Newcombe felt as jittery out there as they would have, and the more grateless of them booed him, forgetting in a twinkling about the 27–7 season that had made this wretched event possible, or the many invitations to choke that Newk had declined along the way and over the years. In a fair world, Newcombe and his teammates should have been allowed to go to these fans' offices the next day and boo *them* every time they made a mistake, just to see how long they could hold a pencil steady —but "That's different" the fans would have said, "being booed goes wit' da territory if you're a ballplayer," just as being stuck with swords is all part of a bull's life in the south of Spain.

By chance, Newcombe did have a rare shot at such vengeance that very afternoon, but I doubt it made him feel any better. By chance a garage attendant with a death wish, and clearly one of life's winners, was waiting in the vicinity of Newk's car to bestow one last boo on him. Newcombe, we can assume, was in something close to tears by then (according to Milton Gross, the sob sister at the *New York Post,* Don spent the evening drenching handkerchiefs and balling them up helplessly—which, allowing for Gross's exaggeration, means that the subject was not at his absolute best) and Newcombe's alcoholism, as we now know, was already barreling toward the nightmare phase, helped on mightily by afternoons such as this one. So to relieve the tension and break the ice, Don did unto the parking attendant what the Yankees had done unto him, and was on his way.

Later in the post-season, the attendant would try to claim damages and it was probably all the judge could do not to hit him again. No real Dodger fan ever got mad at Newcombe for more than a second. He was built like a hero and his triumphs and sorrows were of the same scale. But whichever it was that day, you were proud just to have someone who looked like that representing you. New-combe was, for Dodger fans, the Pitcher as Duke Snider was the Outfielder and as that anonymous Greek was the Discus Thrower.

And besides, whatever Newk did to the attendant was as nothing compared with what O'Malley was about to do to the rest of us. Nineteen fifty-seven might be listed in history as the year Brooklyn and its diaspora spent on their knees before this monstrous figure, this walking cartoon, begging him to leave us our team. No one after that last defeat had dared to say "Wait till next year"—it was too horrible to contemplate. Wait till last year was more like it: the past was our home now and our consolation and would have to do.

Usually nothing is easier to do in America than to blame "it," anything under the sun, on the politicians. But O'Malley got nowhere with that in this case because, outside of any-thing else, we just didn't like him. The cold inscrutability that he needed for bargaining had merely added a grue-some finishing touch to a naturally unsympathetic person-ality, so that we never even saw him at his best, whatever that might be. All we saw was a somewhat unctuous con man, assuring us, as he gazed out the window, that "his roots were in Brooklyn" but that he might be obliged to consider other possibilities.

Why for Godsake? We were in no mood to be fair about this, so we couldn't even see why our favorite ballpark was no longer good enough for him, let alone why he expected the politicians to give him another one. And meanwhile the politicians seemed to be offering him one anyway—offer-ing him several in fact—and he seemed to be turning them all down capriciously.

Centuries of experience have made our politicians as good at dodging blame as the citizenry is at throwing it, and in fact there probably *was* something wrong with most or all of these offers, if only that it was Robert Moses who seemed to loom at the end of every tunnel waving a rule book. Moses had allowed no room for the Brooklyn Dodgers in his master plan for New York, and neither in his infinitely smaller way had Mayor Robert Wagner, who never saw a landmark, even Penn Station, as lovely as a real estate tax and who had, incidentally, the deadest eyes I've ever seen on a man.

So at least suggests Neil J. Sullivan in his doleful, thorough study, *The Dodgers Move West.* Sullivan's version of O'Malley, cooled by thirty years of history, is less evil than ours and more ordinary, and he's probably right. Few characters in history have proved as villainous under close inspection as a Dodger fan's version of Walter O'Malley, which was inflated even beyond its rich deserts by the outsized artificial emotions of sports—that is, we hated him on his merits but we also hated him in the crazy way we "hated" the Giants.

But what shines through even Sullivan's "che sarà, sarà," Brooklyn-was-doomed-anyway account is how easily O'Malley was discouraged, shying away from the smallest obstacles that Moses placed in his path—quibbles that Moses himself would have bowled through without even seeing them if their cases had been reversed. And if Moses couldn't come up with some objection, Walter would do it himself, finding no end of trouble with the right of eminent domain or rejecting outright the site of the future Shea Stadium.

The overpowering impression remains that we were right the first time, minus the horns and tail. O'Malley was a perfectly human sort of monster who simply wanted to go West because that was where the money was. In Los Angeles, the local Moseses and Wagners were not yet jaded with big-league baseball and they seemed to be running with him instead of against him and making him an offer that no banker with a heart of stone could refuse. All they needed to do was dispossess a few peasants and wipe out a whole community (all in a day's work to a Moses on any coast), and the deed was done: Walter O'Malley would have himself a ballpark-plus-surroundings worthy of Louis XIV himself.

Meanwhile, back in the dustbin of history, the East Coast, we were having the kind of miserable, degrading time you get from a leader who doesn't really think public opinion matters, but who keeps on kissing babies and eating pizza anyway. As we watched this very willful man—whose only claim to fame so far had been charging twice for double-headers, or phasing them out altogether, thus increasing attendance figures to modern standards—pause and dither in front of what were to us invisible potholes, his protestations of Brooklyn roots began to take their place among the great villainous quotes of all time. "I have no further territorial ambitions." "Let them eat cake." "I shall never send American boys to fight in [fill in the blank]." O'Malley was right up there.

There is no point, or pleasure, in dwelling on the lame-duck season of 1957. Most of us were watching the clock or the owner's box anyway. The Dodgers really were showing their age out on the field by this time, confirming O'Malley's message of decay. My team is falling apart, can't you see?, just like my ballpark, and knocking the stuffing out of my investment every time it hobbles onto the field. Walter hadn't a moment to lose.

So, like Conrad's *Lord Jim,* he jumped ship and with roughly the same aftermath. As we now know, the Dodgers, sailing under new colors, cruised serenely to another world championship just *two years later.* Walter needn't have hurried after all. The paisanos in Chavez Ravine would have waited. Branch Rickey's old farm system, it turned out, had been humming along quietly all the while, fashioning another fine team right under the old one, and this surfaced in plenty of time to save Walter O'Malley's investment and then some, guaranteeing him an old age spent among his loved ones, dollar bills, which should have more than made up for the loss of his roots in Brooklyn.

"They'll get over it," I can imagine O'Malley saying, and I'm sure, if he'd ever been a fan, *he* would have gotten over it faster than you can say Federal Farm and Sowbellies Exchange. I mean, it wasn't like losing your money. So it would be nice to think that he was at least as impressed as Leona Helmsley might have been by the steadfastness and patience of the hatred his move to L.A. aroused among the little people, a hatred which rages to this day like a fire feeding on itself. It isn't every day that an American citizen finds himself effectively barred from one of our great cities (O'Malley could have returned, but he would have needed an armed guard, and in fact he never bothered)—but then it isn't every day that a city hates someone that much, and who knows what it did to Brooklyn's collective liver to find its love of the Dodgers transformed overnight and forever into a surly unrequited loathing of one fat banker? It was as if the Frank Capra movie O'Malley had been cast for had mysteriously gone wrong, with the banker having the last laugh and Jimmy Stewart deciding to kill himself for real this time, and no airy-fairy nonsense about human goodness winning out in the end.

No one has ever fully gauged, because it is ungaugeable, the part sports teams play in the psychic life of cities. But one knows for sure that if they ever took the Red Sox out of Boston, Beantown would become a different place on the instant, just as surely as if they ripped out the Common or the harbor. The cab drivers would be different, and so would the executives, and the myriad college students who outnumber the stars in the skies in those parts, and so would such simple transactions as trips to the store and just getting up in the morning. This goes way beyond a game you play with a bat and a ball to the very heart of urban life. And this is what O'Malley was messing with—and not because he needed the money. Dodger attendance was still the second best in baseball and he would have made a nice living whatever he'd decided. But an O'Malley can't stop so long as there is a drop of Old Greenback in the house.

"Well, at least you still have the Yankees." One didn't have to be as coldly uncomprehending as O'Malley to say this. In fact, Jimmy Cannon, a New York sportswriter who alternated between wisdom and obtuseness to an extent dizzying even in his profession, wrote a column suggesting that we might as well face the facts and come on over to the only team in town. To this day, I don't know if Cannon was kidding, or if his years in the press box had cut him off from real life and people as completely as life in the front office had O'Malley—or whether, as I suspect, he was just a closet Yankee fan, mocking us in our grief.

Of course, to a genuine Brooklynite, or even a fellow traveler, asking us to come on over to the Yankees was about as consoling as telling a Cub fan that he still had the White Sox. For comparative remoteness, you might as well tell us we had the Moscow Dynamos. There are spiritual distances greater than physical ones can express, and the trip across the East River is one of them. The simple truth was that Brooklyn, which had been one of the founding fathers of the National League before the New York Highlanders had even been thought of, let alone the Yankees that the Highlanders later became, was now without a team. For the first time in living or dead memory. Period.

But if O'Malley and his people, whom I took to be little

windup O'Malleys scampering around at his feet like the toys in the old *New Yorker* cartoon, ever did absorb quite what they have done to the ancient city of Brooklyn, it only served to make them meaner, not mellower. As if to prove this, and to declare themselves true sons of O'Malley, his successors did something in 1990 so mean and small that Scrooge would have wired his congratulations. They sued an amiable establishment in Bay Ridge called the *Brooklyn Dodger Saloon* for infringement of copyright because "Dodger" was *their* name now, as if the ancient Brooklyn art of dodging trolleys could be transferred intact to the Orangeblossom Thruway like a movie set going from MGM to Paramount.

As the commercial used to say, "Thanks, I needed that." Brooklyn fans, like most baseball fans, are incurably sentimental and a few of the Irish brothers may have been tempted to backslide a bit over the years in respect to a man with the fine name of O'Malley. Perhaps there was good and bad on both sides of de ting. If so, here was the slap in the chops they needed to come to their senses. Anyone who thought you could patent a notion like "the Brooklyn Dodgers" and stuff it into your briefcase and park it by your swimming pool was capable of anything.

By chance I myself had received the same message, like a personally engraved pink slip, from the Los Angeles Dodgers just a year before. A friend of mine in publishing had been negotiating with that organization over a centennial book to celebrate the history of the team from year one, and had suggested me as a possible author. And so far I had not been shot down. Although I could think immediately of several writers better grounded in the subject, and even one or two who might not resent the move to LA as much as I did, the little O'Malleys probably couldn't because people like that have never heard of any writers at all

("If we can't get Harold Robbins, I don't know *what* to suggest"). And the lawyers, bless them, were said to be positively enthusiastic (I've always liked lawyers).

Time, obviously, for some soul searching of a kind sports doesn't usually require of you. My subject was simply to be the team on the field, which, so far as I would be concerned, had magically relocated itself one day brick for brick, like the Holy House of Loreto, thousands of miles from home and without human intervention. This is not such a hard leap for a baseball fan—it's a lot easier than crossing that East River—and if I did decide to go west with the Dodgers, I wouldn't be the first old fan to do so.

So did I really hate the team, or just the suits upstairs? While I was feverishly adding up the pluses, I found myself returning again and again to Sandy Koufax and the wonderful World Series of 1963, and counting it twice or three times. That Series would have washed away O'Malley's sins if anything could have. We remembered Sandy ourselves as a gawky kid around the neighborhood, forever throwing on the sidelines and into the stands alternately—fast of course, but Rex Barney had been fast. Lots of guys were fast. All we knew for sure was that the kid would never be another Karl Spooner.

And here he was back, all grown up and smoother than Adolphe Menjou himself. So smooth that you wondered how hard he could throw if he really tried. So smooth that Bobby Richardson, the Yankee contact hitter, fell on his face swinging at his motion and the swooping curve that came out of it, causing old Dodger fans to laugh with excitement. "Hey, this is rich—come on over and see what Koufax is doing to the Yankees." Five strikeouts in a row in the first two innings. "Mantle looked awful, but you really should have seen Richardson."

At the end of the afternoon, Koufax had piled up 15

strikeouts, a World Series record, and all we knew was that he was still wearing a shirt that said *Dodgers* and was cut the old way, and a blue hat, and that for a couple of hours nothing had changed. Johnny Roseboro, wearing the same beautiful outfit, had bashed a three-run home run off Mr. Slick himself, Whitey Ford, in the second inning, and after five innings we had the pleasure of seeing Whitey removed from the game altogether. Well all right—let's have a little humiliation for Ford too while we're about it. And let's get old Tommy Henrich in here, and Dickey and Gomez. Maybe we can even get DiMaggio to throw to the wrong base before this thing is over.

It was the afternoon of the long knives, and there was more where it came from. The next day it would be Johnny Podres, Brooklyn's first and only certified Yankee killer, doling out the medicine, to make it two in a row at the Stadium. Hey, this was easy, why hadn't we thought of it sooner? Maury Wills had opened Game 2 by stealing second while Al Downing thought he was picking him off first. So much for Yankee dignity. Why had we ever been afraid of these guys?

(If we'd known then that the Yankees were about to drop dead of old age themselves two years later, would it have mattered? Two years is a long time in baseball, buster. Just two years before, Mantle and Maris had hit 115 home runs between them, and they still looked the same to me. Now please don't interrupt again.)

The next game, out on the Coast, was all Don Drysdale's, which brought us round to Koufax again. At this point Mel Allen, the braying Yankee announcer, apparently became so overcome with grief that he overdosed badly on cold medicine or whatever, and his announcing of the fourth and last game placed the final cap and bells on Yankee pride. "Hey, how many plates are they using today, Mel?" cackled the merry fellows I was watching with. "So—don't worry about it, Mel, the umps *always* use three thumbs for the final game."

Any decent baseball fan should be content to accept whatever explanation Mel now offers for that performance because (a) no drunk could have lasted as long and as well as he has, and (b) the game was played at noon West Coast time, and (c) Allen's style always sounded kind of woozy and off the wall anyway. But there was something about the way he said "Ask the man for Ballantine—mmm good" as he held up his seventh-inning beer that brought down the house that day. "It's three-ring time!" said Mel, beaming wildly. "Purity, Body, and Flavor!" "How many rings was that, Mel?" said we, collapsing in mirth one more time.

From where we sat (on the floor shaking), getting pie-eyed would have seemed a perfectly loyal and honorable response to what happened to the Yankees that October. In that last game, Joe Pepitone, the comic-opera first baseman of the Yanks, had actually given the game a Dodger touch by losing a throw in the shirts behind third base, for pete-sake—an excuse that not even Billy Loes had thought of. And that was all the Yankees did all day, as Koufax cut their furious bats up in thin slices once again. So Allen, who dated back to Gordon and Keller, had every reason to reach for the Ballantine.

But his bosses didn't see it that way. The Yankees had suits too—charcoal gray with pinstripes—and suits do not come equipped with memories. So Mel Allen was forcibly retired that winter before he could manhandle another game and just like that, thousands of games of yeoman service were flushed away forever. Mel was actually getting out just in time. The glory days were all but over, and his ejection from the premises turned out to be a kindness, like

being hurled roughly into one of the lifeboats on the *Ti-
tanic.* So Mel's career was never tainted with failure.

As for the Yankees, the departure of Allen actually quick-
ened one's sense of rout, like a fire sale. In the interests of
polishing their image, Yankee management was polishing it
out of existence. Getting rid of Allen was equivalent to the
Wizard of Oz throwing out his microphone. The teams that
the Yankees would be fielding from now on would not be
needing it.

However, the Yankees were not my problem right now,
but finding something to like about the Los Angeles
Dodgers, and after 1963 this became difficult. By that time,
the New York Mets were in business, if you could call it
that, leeching off what was left of my baseball time (like
many a Dodger fan, I went into a long slump after 1958),
and I didn't give much of a damn what happened when the
Dodgers got in the Series again in 1965 and '66. They
weren't playing the Yankees any more, those days were over
for good, it was official, and my feelings about the Twins
and Orioles remind me of Muhammad Ali's famous phrase,
"I ain't got nothin' against them Viet Cong." These Twins
and the O's were, after all, none other than born-again versions of the old Washington Senators and St. Louis Browns,
my old playmates from Philadelphia days in the American
League cellar. By the seventies, the Athletics themselves
would be joining them both in *their* latest incarnation, and
that decade would be dominated by the two teams I had
seen first in the mythical season of 1941. The Brownies and
the A's. Only in America.

These facts were interesting in the sense that the hiero-
glyphs in a pyramid are interesting—quaint, but not grip-
ping—and I cite them principally to show how easily my
attention was and is distracted from the Los Angeles
Dodgers.

Refocusing sternly, one comes to the beautiful seventh game of the 1965 Series, between Koufax again and Jim Kaat, with Koufax quivering like a greyhound who has a lot of run in him today, a perfect mixture of eagerness and poise, and Kaat volleying back hard like a tough Dutch sailor. 2–0. A gem. We'll certainly feature that in our Dodger book.

Not so the 1966 World Series. That was the one where the Dodgers were allegedly bleeped off because the little dears were being obliged to go to Japan in the off-season, where they would presumably be forced into hot tubs by ruthless geisha girls. I preferred to think at the time that they were simply rebelling against management high-handedness, but either way it was a pleasure to see the old Brownies give them their lumps in four straight. The thought of going to Japan seemed to press particularly hard on Willie Davis, who lost two easy fly balls in the sun, a rarity in those days when players were used to daylight, to sabotage Koufax in the second game and end my effective interest in the Series. Interviewed after the game, Davis said that his errors were "no big deal"; and if they were all right with him, they were certainly all right with me.

By the time the Dodgers got back into a championship I had been born again myself as a Met fan in the crucible of the 1969 season, but I guess I rooted for the Dodgers in the mildest possible sense of the word when they played against the Oakland A's in 1974 (no champions should dress like that) and more vehemently when they met George Steinbrenner's bought-again Yankees in '77, '78, and '81. But my chief memory of even those Series was not of any Dodger triumphs but of my car battery going dead just as Reggie Jackson stuck out his hip and got hit with a throw and—huh? *What happened?* Let's roll it back to 1963, shall we?

It was a thin collection, but the book offer had given me a welcome chance to review it and contemplate the way one gradually severs connections with a favorite team, an old love, while hanging on to one's early memories of it.

And that's all the book offer did give me. Because before I had time to weigh what effect the Hershiser World Series might have on the scales, or how much the pleasure of being paid to see ball games was worth, or more profoundly, how one compared sporting fickleness with real-life betrayals, word came from the Coast that there was a slight hitch.

It turned out that the Dodgers hadn't realized that you were supposed to *pay* authors for their work and were having a bit of trouble with the idea. Ballplayers, they understood, had to be paid—quite a lot, actually—but *writers?* What could they do for you? Since the advance we were suggesting wouldn't have kept a utility infielder in meal money, it must have been the principle of the thing, because as it transpired, they didn't want to pay any advance at all. They planned, in that championship year, to celebrate 100 great years of Dodger history by signing up the first writer who agreed to write about it for nothing.

It was a merciful release. I believe it was the splendid comedian Joe E. Lewis who said that "if you lend a friend ten bucks and never see him again, it was worth it." And that's pretty much how I felt and feel about the Los Angeles Dodgers. It would have been a nice assignment, but not having to gild these creeps, or ever think about them again, is a lot nicer: it felt as if a novel that had dragged on much too long had, just like that, ended itself perfectly. And the satisfaction should be good for a lifetime.

11

Born Again

My years in the wilderness between the Dodgers and the
first Mets team that came close enough to a pennant race to
justify serious rooting broadened my baseball base to the
point of insipidity: I was a fan of the game itself now, adopt-
ing various teams for a few years, like an uncle taking a
niece to tea at the Plaza.

The Pirates with Bob Clemente and Dick Groat and
Don Hoak, the ex–Brooklyn Dodger and prototypical baseball rowdy, were a team I had to like if only for the part
they played in maybe the best World Series game ever
played from-the-point-of-view-of-people-who-had-to-work-

in-offices-that-day, a category that has since been retired for good in favor of night games played in hoar-frost for couch potatoes fighting sleep. At the place where I worked that year, I remember us taking ever more rapid turns going downstairs for coffee, so we could come back with the latest bulletin—and everyone returning with a fresh wonder story as if we were trying to top each other. Rocky Nelson did this, Yogi Berra did that. Tell me another one. By the end, memory insists that we'd found a radio somewhere— but if there's one thing this book has taught me, it is how often memory can get things just slightly wrong. Anyway, it was back to radio days that afternoon, with one's imagination overheating wildly from working so hard. I could swear, for instance, that I *saw* Mazeroski's game-winning home run—although for a split second I also thought I saw a clump of ivy on the wall before I remembered that they didn't have ivy at Forbes Field. So I *un*saw it, and saw it again.

The Pirates would continue to be favorites of mine until they took to wearing those ridiculous uniforms in the seventies, and I was happy to run across them one March in Bradenton, where I sat a couple of times with the old-timers in the fishing caps watching the Bucs go through the blithe motions of spring training, smiling, some of them, for the last time all year. I particularly liked the way Clemente would perch in the rear outside corner of the batter's box, as far from the plate as the law allowed, and "give" the pitcher the outside inch of the plate—if he could take it. (Clemente's dexterity with the bat, like Matty Alou's, reminded me of cricket, and of what great cricketers the Caribbean has produced. In spring training, the fan also wool-gathers.)

The difference between an acquired taste like the Pirates

and an aged-in-the-wood one like the Brooklyn Dodgers is that you're not willing to plunge to the bottom with the new guys, but are soon whoring after new contenders to love. If you can't have a real team of your own, you can at least have a pennant race every year. And since there was no compelling reason to hate the Cardinals any more, and they seemed to be the new girls in town once again, I took the opportunity to enjoy the sheer ferocity of Bob Gibson on the mound and the smoothness of Bill White and the everything of Lou Brock, speed and power, the first guy you'd pick for a playground game. That was a great team, and the correct one, now that the Dodgers and Giants had defected, to drive the final nail into the Yankees' coffin in 1964.

But even this was not enough to keep me from taking a thimbleful of pleasure from the Tiger victory over the Cards in 1968. By this time, playing the field had left me as wishy-washy as one of those kibitzers who drops by to ask "What's the score, who's playing?"—I wanted the Cardinals to win that year, but if they didn't, well, Al Kaline was a great player too, and let's hear it for Mickey Lolich.

It was cool communication—so cool that my wife and I had taken the children to Spain the year Roger Maris hit all those home runs and I hadn't missed it *too* much. Real life will make no further inroads into this book, but there was a lot of other stuff going on around then besides baseball, and for several years it was possible to believe the outside world was the real one and baseball was the dream.

It was obviously high time to settle down and get serious. My old friend Joe Flaherty used to say that you're not a fan if you don't have a team, and I had begun stepping out in a desultory sort of way with the New York Mets, more for convenience than anything else, like an Irish courtship. But in 1969, it burst into flame and treated me to the kind of rejuvenation that a sports fan can receive at any time in his life and is perhaps the best justification one can give for our peculiar hobby.

In the fall of 1969, *Sports Illustrated* asked me if I'd like to take a whirl at reviewing sports on TV for them. As part of the deal, I asked if they could see their way to giving me a TV set that worked, and my state-of-the-art Zenith arrived just in time for the third game of the 1969 World Series.

There are certain days that go straight up on the wall in your den, days that step out of the pack and announce that they're on their way to the Hall of Fame for Good Days. I had just spoken briefly at a peace rally for publishers, than whom there is no one more peaceful to begin with, and the sun had smiled, the crowd had smiled, and there was an October tingle in the air of a kind that New York knows how to take and run with. I promised no more real world, but there was absolutely nothing real about this. Somebody seemed to have fed the audience laughing gas and the happy publishers could barely suppress a chuckle even at the speakers who pretended to be angry (I assumed they were pretending). It was such a great day to get out of the office that we could have been talking about anything.

Then home lickerty-lip in time to see Tommie Agee lead off for the Mets in the bottom half of the first inning on what would be his day of days too, twenty-four hours of unambiguous glory in a patchy, disappointing career. So naturally he led off with a home run. But hitting wasn't the half of it for Agee today. What would get him into the great newsreel in the sky for as long as it runs were two catches of a kind that make you drop your glass and spill ash on your vest—one to his right and one to his left, as if he were modeling catches on a runway.

But then, as if to confirm the pixilated quality of the day, the real hitting star of the game turned out to be not Agee at all but an .081 hitter on the year named Gary Gentry, who also pitched just fine, allowing for the fact that he had Tommie Agee in back of him, not to mention God on his side. Since Gentry would soon be succumbing to a sore arm, a plague that snatches young pitchers from sight as if they'd never been born, he more than anyone must have rejoiced to have this game on his chart for all time.

Once you know that you've been predestined for salvation, the rest is a formality. So it seemed quite to be expected that the oafish Ron Swoboda would suddenly take it into his head to fly through the air like a swallow to snag a line drive off Brooks Robinson to break the back of an Oriole rally and lead the Mets to victory in game 4.

And we had to smother our yawns by the time a utility infielder named Al Weis, who would retire with a lifetime total of seven regular-season home runs, decided to pop one over the fence in the fifth and last game, tying the score and leaving the Orioles talking to themselves from that day to this. There was no point in their trying anything else— the Mets would only counter it with something equally ridiculous. When you're in the magician's cave you just want to get out as quickly as possible before he turns you into bubble-gum, and we heard no more from the Baltimores in the last couple of innings.

So I had me a new team and a second wind, and have lived happily cum grouchily ever after. But who wants to hear about the home life of Ulysses? The Mets and I have had our ups and downs since then, but we don't discuss them in the public prints (though why oh why did they have to let all those pitchers go in the Viola trade?). The story ends, purely as a story, the moment Cleon Jones catches the last fly ball and sinks to one knee in the briefest of genuflections before facing the oncoming delirious mob.

The fact that the ball was hit by Davey Johnson might be the start of another story, but not this one.

That afternoon, with the shadows lengthening, cheerfully for once, over our little miracle, baseball was giving us all it had to give. And it was plenty.